Reviews for Nomad

'Alan Partridge's *Nomad* is almost certainly the funniest book ever written'   Caitlin Moran

'Funniest book of the year'   *Sunday Telegraph*

'Bathos is everywhere. It's glorious'   Sam Leith, *Guardian*

'Overwrought, fanatically detailed, unhinged – and utterly hilarious. A must'   Alice Jones, *i News*

'Sensationally funny. What brilliant writing'   Richard Osman

'An uproariously funny read, with genius jokes on every page'   *Heat*

'Sensational'   Jenny Colgan

'Hilarious'   Jon Ronson

'[*Nomad*] is, if you need me to tell you, hilarious'   *Choice*

'Brilliantly funny'   Marcus Brigstock

'Partridge fans will love it'   *Financial Times*

Alan Partridge

NOMAD

NOMAD

ALAN PARTRIDGE

With Rob Gibbons, Neil Gibbons and Steve Coogan

TRAPEZE

A TRAPEZE PAPERBACK

First published in Great Britain in 2016
by Trapeze
This paperback edition published in 2017
by Trapeze,
an imprint of Orion Publishing Group Ltd,
Carmelite House, 50 Victoria Embankment,
London EC4Y 0DZ

An Hachette UK company

5 7 9 10 8 6 4

A CIP catalogue record for this book
is available from the British Library.

ISBN: 978 1 40915 671 0

Typeset by Input Data Services Ltd, Bridgwater, Somerset

Printed in Great Britain by Clays Ltd, St Ives plc

MIX
Paper from
responsible sources
FSC® C104740

www.orionbooks.co.uk

nomad

/ˈnəʊmad/

noun

1 a person who does not stay long in the same place; a wanderer.

2 a member of a people that travels from place to place to find fresh pasture for its animals and has no permanent home.*

3 *Scottish*: 'not mad'.

*The author would like to point out that he does have a permanent home.

CONTENTS

***

ACKNOWLEDGEMENTS

***

On this occasion there is no one I wish to acknowledge.
Thank you.

to walk
to trek
to hike
to yomp

to amble
to ramble
to womble
to wander

(to slither
both hither
and thither)

to march
to mince
to trudge
to traipse

to stroll
to stride
to stomp
to STOP

'Getting About' by A. G. Partridge, aged nineteen

PROLOGUE:

WHAT I TALK ABOUT WHEN
I TALK ABOUT RAMBLING

***

PUMFF. A FOOT IS DOLLOPED onto the ground. In under a second it is load-bearing, locking in place to become a willing pivot for the body as a whole. It accepts the load dutifully, bending a little at the knee in a small act of genuflection. Above it, a roll of the hips tells the trailing leg to scramble and it responds by hoisting itself aloft and catapulting its cargo (the other foot) forwards. This foot reaches out and finds land. Pumff. Then it too locks in place and takes the weight of its owner before silently passing the centre of gravity back to its counterpart like an Olympic torch made of physics.

This transaction is repeated, back and forth, back and

forth, and it's soon clear that this tandem act is propelling the whole unit forwards in fluid locomotion.

What I've just described might sound complex, but it's not a newly invented dance or corporate team-building activity, it's something we all[1] do every single day. Give up?

I'm talking . . . about *walking*. Because this book is *about* walking.

Yes, walking. 'Oh,' some of you are saying. 'I don't walk. I'm not a walker.' Oh really? Then how did you get to the bathroom for your morning toilet? How did you make it from your house to your car? How did you get from the door of the newsagent's to the freezer where they keep the Magnums (Magna)? Perhaps you slithered there? Or was it teleportation? No. You walked, mate. Accept it. Because we all walk. All of us.[2]

It's an activity that has been part of our lives for so long we take it for granted. A walk can be as humdrum as strolling to the larder to grab a plate of eggs or popping from your desk to a colleague's desk to tell her to turn her music down. It can be as emotional as walking down a church aisle, to give away a daughter at her wedding or bear a pall at a funeral. Our walks are as unique as we are – from the pert strut of a Strictly Come Dancer to the no-nonsense galumph of a Tory lady politician. Yes, walking has been with us for some time and looks set to stay with us for many more years to come.

When I stroll, my heart swells, my mind races, my soul

---

1 Not all.

2 With some exceptions.

soars. For that is the power of walking. It doesn't just transport us, it *transports* us – which I know is the same word twice, but the second time should be said louder and slower.

When I promenade, I am overcome with gratitude. Not for the scenery – the UK Highways Agency and our obsession with 'affordable housing' have seen to that – but for my own legs. Legs are the heroes of walking. They are among the largest limbs on the human body, comprising an average of 45 per cent of our overall length, and yet so little is known about them. What I can say is that these dignified, uncomplaining peninsulas are integral to walking. I'll go further: they are essential. These are my steeds, my ferrymen, and they deliver me onwards.

And with that thought tumbling round your head like hiking socks in a washing machine, please enjoy this book.

Alan Partridge, August 2016

1.

COLD OPENING

***

FOUR MINUTES. Four minutes to save East Anglia.

Four minutes. Just 240 seconds. I look at my watch, and in slow motion I mouth the word 'Moooooootherrrrrfuuuuuck-errrrrrrr' (motherfucker). The brow of the hill is still some way away and the bald facts are these: I have just four minutes to make it to the top or I risk the lives of hundreds, if not thousands, of men, women and children. People will die.

My feet pound the asphalt, really giving the popular road surface what for. Wham, wham, wham, wham. The cat's eyes peer back at me, as if the frightened earth is peeping out at its punisher from beneath a tarmac duvet.

Wham, wham, wham, wham. Want more, do you? Wham, wham, wham, wham.

I pick up the pace. Another check of my watch. Sixty seconds, forty-five seconds. Twenty seconds.

I'm so close I can almost smell the hill's brow.

Ten seconds, five seconds. Three seconds. One second. Half a second. A quarter of a second. A fifth of a second is all that stands between triumph and disaster. Ten metres to go. A sixth of a second remains. Five metres. Exactly one seventh of a second left. Two metres. My calves are so distressed they're almost mooing, like their farmyard name-sakes. Just one-hundredth of a second and then . . . YES!

I've done it. I've done it. *East Anglia is saved.* I look down from the hilltop at Norfolk, silently weeping for the lives that were so close to being snuffed from us. They shall never know how close they came to death. For I have reached a roadside bench atop a hill, from where I can look down on Suffolk, literally as well as metaphorically.

Right on cue, the clouds give way and beams of sunlight fire through them, as if God is trying to laser off an unsightly tattoo (Suffolk). Having saved so many souls, I am overcome with a full-body euphoria and I realise I'm celebrating, jumping up and down, arms aloft, like Rambo on the steps of Philadelphia town hall.

And then: sandwiches.

***

As the tuna-and-sweetcorn filling explodes in my grateful mouth, I reflect on what has just happened. In reality, of course, no lives were at risk. And even if they had been I could have done little or nothing to help them. So what gived?

Well, what I've just been describing was little more (little more!) than a stunningly effective motivational technique. I'm attempting a long walk and I find I'm able to cover great distances by dividing the journey up into chunks, telling myself they have to be completed in a certain (arbitrary) time frame, and attributing grave consequences to failure.

It's a technique I pioneered in primary school. 'Climb to the top of this rope or Grandad kills himself.' 'Catch the ball three times in a row or you contract herpes.' And in this case, 'Get to the brow of that hill in four minutes or Norfolk is destroyed by an insane billionaire who is ready to detonate a subterranean munitions dump hidden beneath the county and blow the landmass sky-high.'

And it's working. Yes, I sometimes have to artificially elongate the final second by splitting it into half, a third or hundredths of a second and counting them slowly, but I'm chipping away at the walk. And God Christ, it needs chipping away at. The Footsteps of My Father Walk is 160 miles long.

I look ahead to the brow of the next hill, and the sunlight lasers into my eyes. I allow them both to squint, the bony caves of my eye sockets narrowing a little, as if they're each trying to grip an ill-fitting monocle. I enjoy this expression. The seriousness of the frown percolates down into my body and I feel more Dimbleby than ever.

I fix my gaze on the horizon, or just past it, lean into the wind and begin to stride towards it, desperate to get there in six minutes to prevent the Duke and Duchess of Cambridge from being simultaneously beheaded with one long sword. I am Alan Partridge. I am under a little pressure but I am focused and happy.

2.

WHAT HAS *DRIVEN* ME TO WALK

***

'WILL THEY BE TAKING ME for lunch? I've forgotten my toothpicks.'

'The letter just said "an invitation to pitch ideas".'

It's six weeks earlier and I'm sitting in the passenger seat of my own car while my assistant drives it (badly). Usually this would irritate me immensely, her hunched seating position a painful indication of how much she's fiddled with my carefully calibrated seat settings. But today she can adjust the steering column and even angle the wing mirrors if she likes (as long as she doesn't fiddle with the three preprogrammed seating positions, which I've named cruise, rally and service station kip, or SSK), because I am extremely upbeat. My destination: the British Broadcasting Corporation (BBC). My task: to pitch some ideas at commissioners who have responded to my assistant's mail-drop by calling me in to hear more.

It's an unexpected invitation for a presenter pushing sixty, sure. But Yewtree has been a Night of the Long Knives for broadcasters of a certain age and has left a hole in the roster of greying presenters that not even that woman who sued *Countryfile* could fill.

'Did they seem pleased I was coming?'

'It was just a PA,' says my assistant, her face so close to the windscreen her breath keeps fogging it up.

'PAs can sound pleased,' I tell her. Just because she's been grumpy ever since her mum died intestate, it doesn't mean she should tar other administrators with the same grey brush. 'Stop the car!'

My assistant slams on the brakes, her one and only method of braking, in all honesty. (She really doesn't have gentle feet, lacking what I call 'chiropodal dexterity'.) Still, we're stationary now and I exit the vehicle just outside the Beeb, telling her I'll meet her in there. There's someone else I've just spotted, across the road from Broadcasting House, about to enter the Langham Hotel:[3] Julia Bradbury.

There's always been a certain frisson between Bradbury and me. I've said on air many times what an accomplished

---

3 Never stayed there myself. It's always seemed a bit 'jazz hands' with its overelaborate cream teas and the cost of G&Ts comfortably in double figures.

and attractive presenter she is, and she sent me a lovely message when I posted her a copy of my memoir, *I, Partridge*, then texted to make sure it had arrived: 'Got your book, thanks.'

I bound from the car, noticing she's with short-haired presenter Clare Balding and a well-oiled gentleman. All three are in high spirits.

'Hi, it's Alan! Great to see you,' I shout from across the road. But they don't hear me over the traffic that clogs up every road in the city. People always tell you the streets are paved with gold in London; they don't say you'll need to lift a bus out of the way to get at it.

I jog over the road and say, 'Hi, it's Alan! Great to see you.' But they're deep in conversation.

'Julia'll tell you,' the man is saying to Balding. 'Move from the BBC to Channel 4 and the whole set-up is different . . .'

'Oh, very different. *Very* different!' I say, deciding to join in that way.

The three of them stop to look at me. 'Hi, it's Alan! Great to see you,' I say.

'Hi, Alan,' says Julia.

Silence. But I'm happy to fill silence, always have been.

'Two very distinct ethoses,' I continue.

'How so?' says Balding, whose surname, up close, is revealed to be a total misnomer. Her hair is in wonderful, thick condition.

'Well, Channel 4 shows start with "A Very British" and the BBC's start with "The Great British". Two very different approaches to British TV.'

They look at me, hesitantly. I elaborate.

'*Coup, Brothel, Sex Scandal, UFO Hoax*,' I say, listing the 'Very British' Channel 4 progs on my left hand. Then I raise my right. '*Menu, Bake Off, Railway Journeys, Sewing Bee.*'

I open my hands as if to say, 'And there you have it,' silently mouthing the words by accident and wincing at myself for doing so.

'Harvey Kennedy,' says the man, shaking my hand. 'Funny, I did a little bit on *Railway Journeys* . . .'

'More than a little bit,' scoffs Balding, her hair becoming fuller and more lustrous every time I look at it.

'Well, yes,' he replies. 'I represent Portillo. Michael and I took it to the channel. Seven series and five books later, here we are.' He smiles. Well, you would.

'He got me the *Ramblings* gig on Radio 4 and we've done one hundred and sixty-seven episodes!' says Balding. Man, that *hair*.

'One hundred and sixty-seven? Why have I never heard of it?' I say, before realising it's because I don't listen to Radio 4.

'And Julia's done *Wainwright's Walks, Railways Walks, Canal Walks, Icelandic Walks*,' continues Balding or Balding continues. 'Harvey's got her walking all the way to the bank.'

'Who commissioned that? Let me guess, Channel 4.'

'No, I just mean she's doing well financially.'

'Oh, I see,' I say, laughing at the idea of Julia Bradbury presenting a show in which she walks from her house to the bank. Can you imagine! Although I *would* watch it.

'What can I say, people love a journey,' laughs Harvey. The ladies laugh. Sod it, I laugh.

Suddenly, Portillo is standing there, all pink trousers and that facial expression that looks like he's smiling but is actually just the way his features hang.[4]

'What is this? Some sort of Walkers' Lunch?' I laugh. They smile at me benignly, meaning yes.

'Shall we . . .?' Portillo says, and they turn to the hotel.

'I love a journey!' I blurt out. 'Has anyone ever walked the M12 route? Motorway proposed in the 1960s between the M11 and Brentwood. Never built but a fascinating insight into urban pla—'

'Nice to meet you, Alan,' smiles Harvey.

'Or east to west across England's narrowest point? The Beltline of Britain. Or just a rectangle around the Midlands. I'd call that one The Guts of Albion.'

'It helps if it has some historical or personal significance, you know,' says Harvey Kennedy, and he pats my shoulder as if to say, 'I like you, Alan.'

By now, my assistant is phoning me repeatedly so I thank them for their chats, have a quick final glance at Bradbury, then a quick final glance at Balding's hair. And I'm off, ready to pitch the living hell out of my id-port (ideas portfolio).

***

On my arrival at Broadcasting House, the PA doesn't sound pleased – but then nor would I if I had to appear in the background on BBC News every time I popped to the lavatory. Speaking of which, I tell my assistant to keep them

---

4 Geoffrey Hayes from TV's *Rainbow* suffered from the same thing.

talking while I pop to a cubicle to psyche myself up. Not that I need to do much psyching. I've been summoned. They asked for me. I am so pumped.

Once fully, fully razzed, I stride out, and through the door, next to which my assistant is looking concerned.

I'm met by a depressing scene. A room full of 100, maybe 200 people, none of them over thirty-five. An absolute *phalanx* of young TV types armed with PowerPoint presentations who are firing off buzzwords like there's no tomorrow, which for them I dearly hope there isn't. One man wearing a fisherman's woolly hat is on a raised stage saying something about 'a fashion programme for the discerning mature gent', adding that it's 'more George Clooney than George Lazenby'. Everyone laughs. But I once shared a paella with George Lazenby and don't.

I turn to my assistant. 'I thought this was meant to be a one-on-one meeting. This is an open day.'

'I'd have to check the letter.'

'Check your eyes, woman. It is an open day. It's clearly an open day.'

Not to worry! And with that, we bob out of the door and head back to Norfolk (I drive), where the only people who wear fishermen's hats are the trawlermen at Brancaster, all the while discussing potential competition ideas for *Mid Morning Matters*, the digital radio show that keeps me both happy and fulfilled and content.

***

Late that night, however, I lie awake and realise I, Alan Partridge, am in the grip of a grump.

It's nothing to do with the absence of telly work. It's not. I couldn't give a shit about that.

No, for days, or is it weeks now, I've been sleepwalking.[5] I'm on autopilot. Days spool by like biz-cards on a Rolodex. I've been absentminded, the quick snap of my synapses dulled, sudokus left unnumbered. I'm making uncharacteristic (and unforgivable) mind-lapses: parking in a standard space instead of the disabled bay – *completely forgetting* my assistant is in the car and carries her blue badge with her; opening a new adventure playground and forgetting to thank the mayor. I'd thanked the kids who'd helped build and paint it, of course I had, everyone had. But failing to formally offer thanks to an elected official of the council, resplendent in his gown and chain? Well, that's just not Alan Partridge. I always thank the mayor, and, save this one unfortunate oversight, I hope to always thank the mayor.

This ennui has even infected my professional life. My

---

5 Now that's not a phrase anyone would associate with Alan Partridge. Not least because I've been outspoken in my doubts about sleepwalking. I'm what you might term a somnambusceptic. Don't believe in it. I just don't buy it. I know some people do – you, the reader, might – but I don't. It's stupid and I'm just not having it. Sure, you might roll over in your sleep or fiddle with your nutsack, but walking? No. The whole thing is a smokescreen, a get-out-of-jail-free card, and just doesn't stand up to any scrutiny. Raided the fridge when you're supposed to be on a diet? Sleepwalking. Took a hammer to a much-loved CD collection? Sleepwalking. Found in the spare room with your colleague Philip, after your husband had let him stay over because he'd had two glasses of wine and was over the limit even though they were small glasses and he was clearly fine to drive? Sleepwalking. Come off it, Carol.

broadcasting is lacking the pep, the zip, the scriff,[6] the wizzle[7] that until now it has always delivered.

Yes, there is a hole in me. I don't mean the physical holes – the mouth, the nostrils, the ears or the other two – this is a hole at my very core. A soul hole.

Truth is, I've been this way for some time. I am not at peace. I feel listless, but why? I make a list of possible causes, and yet even with this list, I remain listless. Is that even possible? To have a list and still be listless? Either way, it bugs the bleeding shit of me![8]

Yes, I am very much in the doldrums, the doldra.

And late that night, it comes to a head.

I'm at Denton Abbey, my Norwich home. Denton Abbey is massive and brilliant. It's the kind of house you drive past and say, 'Shit, who lives there?' Well, I'm delighted to say the shit-who-lives-there is me.[9]

It's 4 a.m. I'm trying to sleep but my mind is troubled. A segment of *The One Show* yesterday evening had looked at

---

6 Check.

7 Check.

8 'Bleeding shit' is merely a turn of phrase. Blood on toilet paper is a common sign of bowel cancer and I check each sheet diligently, aware that if there are dots of red, it's generally nothing more than a rectal fissure. I do not have bowel cancer (or haemorrhoids).

9 I secured finance with the help of a nifty Albanian accountant who drinks at my local pub. By simply using Peartree Productions, its assets and the assets of my guarantor, Lynn Benfield, as collateral, I found a lender who was happy to back me. Monthly repayments are a cinch and so long as the pipeline of income doesn't let up even for a moment, there'll be no problem whatsoever.

heat loss in large houses, making its point using a thermal-imaging camera so that the hot air escaping the roof looked like a red biro leaking ink into an upside-down shirt pocket.

The report was fronted by Dom Littlewood, a presenter who looks and sounds like he won his primetime BBC One presenting job in a raffle (and probably did). He finished with a to-camera piece in which, clutching a wad of cash, he suggested an uninsulated homeowner was wasting 'pound . . . [throwing a banknote away] . . . after pound [he threw another one], after pound [and another]'.

This too has annoyed me. Throwing the note on the word 'pound' seemed to suggest that the note represented a pound – singular. But one-pound notes were withdrawn from circulation some thirty years ago. If he'd thrown one-pound coins as he said it, fine. Likewise, if he'd reworded the sentence to say 'pounds upon pounds upon pounds', that would also have worked. But he didn't. He threw a banknote on the word 'pound' and that was wrong. Lazy and wrong.

I'd texted Fernando to see if he was watching. 'No.' I explained my issue to him. 'Fuck's sake, Dad, does it matter?' I'd explained that yes, it did matter, and this time Ferny didn't reply, suggesting he'd changed his mind and now agreed with me.

But still this has riled me and now, hours later, I'm all a-jitter.

The report itself hasn't helped either. I toss and turn, trying against try to forget the upsetting facts and figures, but they swim in front of me like so many curious carps/carp. National Insulation Association figures point to a 66 per cent heat loss through uninsulated solid walls, 25 per cent through the loft/roof space, and 20 per cent through windows and doors. Taken together, it means houses could lose as much as 111 per cent of their heat, and I become angry at the notion of a house losing 11 per cent more heat than it could ever have had in the first place.

I try to put these thoughts from my mind, pledging instead to count sheep. I picture them running across my mind's eye, hurdling a fence gaily before gambolling on. But even this riles me. I think about the fence. What farmer fences off half of his own field? No farmer. So the sheep are either leaping off his property into that of a neighbour or they're jumping back onto his land. In which case, where have they been? Do all sheep do this? Maraud across farmland while the rest of us sleep? If so, why not make the fences higher? It's absolutely idiotic. Another reason to despise farmers.

I stop myself. No more questions, Alan. Just focus on the sheep. And although this relaxes me for a while, I begin to fixate on the fleeces. In my mind, these sheep are clad not in wool but in rockwool lagging, and after clearing the fence they are all leaping into the joists of my neighbour's loft, cutting his heating bills by up to £250 a year.

I get up, and with a grumble and a sniff I make my way to the loft, aware that I won't achieve sleep until I've assessed the loft insulation myself.

My bottom is itchy so I stop in the middle of the landing and scratch it lightly. The fiddling merely tantalises the itch, and it becomes more aggressive. I respond in kind, dragging my fingernails across my fundament in a frenzied jerking motion. With one hand braced against the wall, I'm now grabbing and clawing at the angry aperture, slashing and scraping in a bid to ease the sensation. It's a delicious relief but I know it's merely stoking the irritation. And so after a final flurry – scrit, scrit, scrit, scrit, scit, scrit, scrit, scrit, scrit, scrit, scrit, scrit, scrit, scrit, scrit, scrit, scrit, scrit – I stop scratching. My backside pleads with me to continue but I resist, and in a few seconds the itch subsides on its own, as I knew it would.[10]

I clamber up the loft ladder and grab my torch from just inside the hatch. Like a detective inspecting a murder scene, I pop the torch in my mouth, leaving my hands free for detecting and inspecting. It would work better with a slim pen torch – mine is a fat, heavy-duty Maglite and it stretches my lips painfully, like when the cleaner's not been and there are only serving spoons left – but I press on regardless.

I detect and inspect the roof space, quickly concluding that no, my roof isn't insulated. *The One Show* had asked viewers to get in touch with their thoughts on home insulation so, even though the programme has long finished, I send an SMS to 8882 that reads 'My home isn't insulated.' I'm too late for today's show, but they might read it out at the start of tomorrow's.

As I turn to leave the roof space, I see an old cardboard box, containing various papers, old photos and a length of

---

10 Admittedly, this isn't relevant to the story but I don't believe in flinching from the truth, however unnecessary or unpalatable it might be. Moreover, it all contributes to the word count and there's nothing in my publishing agreement to say what I can and can't fill the book with. I've just realised that the fifth scrit was spelt 'scit'. This was my error and I apologise for it.

tinsel. It seems to look back at me, the perforated hand-hold leering like a mouth. I recognise that leer, but where from?

There's an otherworldliness to this box. I hesitate to describe it as an aura because that's a word generally used by women who work in offices and loudly describe themselves as 'spiritual'. But it's as if the box has a magnetism and my eyes are made of metal. It seems to be calling to me: 'Hey, Alan. Whatcha doing? You wanna look inside of me?' Quite camp but maybe that's the tinsel.

'No,' I say, for some reason out loud.

I'm tired and irritated – what is wrong with me? I pry the torch from my now sore lips, switch it off, and then climb down the loft ladder, jumping the last two steps (as I always do) so I look like Neil Armstrong dismounting the steps of *Eagle*, the Apollo 11 lunar module – not so much a *moon* landing, as *my* landing (my emphasis). I nod appreciatively. 'Nice line, Alan.'

I don't even bother slinking back to bed. I shower up and get ready for work.

***

'Like the name of a cartoon Belgian detective said in a Scottish accent, it's 10:10.'[11]

It's later that morning and I'm ten minutes into my daily radio show *Mid Morning Matters*.[12]

'The song you just heard was "Midnight Train to

---

11 Tintin. Try it!!!

12 For the uninitiated, *Mid Morning Matters* is like Andrew Marr's Sunday morning politics show, but minus the arrogance.

Georgia". The Georgia in America, presumably, rather than the failed Soviet state of the same name – where I'm sure the only "midnight trains" you'd find are the ones taking dissidents to death camps! Still, good song.'

I'm feeling a good deal better. Bright, alert and upbeat enough not to mind that much when my sidekick, Simon Denton, pipes up: 'But whereas she was "Gladys Knight", I'm "glad it's mid-morning" because it means it's time for Your Call.'

It's my job to introduce Your Call. He knows that. Besides, it's a pun that – let's be honest – didn't quite work. In the early days of our working relationship, I would have laughed out of politeness so as not to dent his fragile confidence (I happen to know he grows a full beard to obscure the part of his face that makes him most self-conscious).[13] But as time's gone on, I've realised that he simply won't learn if I indulge him so I now respond to his weaker material by digging my fingernails into his arm or by leaving a few seconds of dead air in which his joke can flap and gasp for breath like a stricken fish.

This time he's not given me that option. He is just out of my nails' range, and dead air might suggest I've forgotten the topic of my own phone-in. So I rise above it and decide that on this occasion I'll show a bit of serenity and simply leave it there. Anyway, I get him later by pushing him at a urinal.

Today's phone-in question is simple: 'What should be the eighth deadly sin?' We all know the seven existing ones:

13 Big jowls.

pride, envy, wrath, gluttony, lust, sloth, etc. But which forms of evil should be added to the list? My suggestions are 'bad hygiene' and 'using rising inflection at the end of a sentence when you're not even asking a question'.

It's good radio and I feel good that it's good. But while the phone-in provokes a range of interesting opinions – 'clumsiness', 'vegetarianism' and 'the sheer indecisiveness of bisexuality' are all solid answers – it soon descends into more trivial territory.[14] Soon enough the topic has been co-opted by chauvinistic tradesmen, who like to call during their lunch breaks,[15] and what began as a thoughtful philosophical debate is now just a list of things they hate about women: 'shrillness', 'watching *Hollyoaks*' and 'taking too long at a cash machine'. This isn't the highbrow debate I'd envisaged.

I make it clear that I find this to be hateful towards women – although they do take too long at cash machines – and deliberately put on a bad record, 'Fairground' by Simply Red. An awful piece of music that I sometimes put on when I want to annoy my own listeners. Simon looks at me as I get up to go. I can tell he's worried – this grumpiness just isn't like me.

I stride out of the studio to go and do, or have, a wee. I barge past Dominic [Don't know his second name], from our advertising sales team.

---

14 Which is usually fine. I'm a *huge* champion of trivial radio and some of my fondest moments in broadcasting, and indeed life, have been utterly, utterly trivial.

15 At about 11:30 a.m. Why do tradesmen do that? Start work at 7 and knock off at 3?

'Ah, just the man,' he says. I walk on.

'Loving the deadly sins chat, Alan! But Pizza Hut have asked if you can paint gluttony in a more positive light as it's central to their business model. And they are an advertiser, so . . .'

I ignore him.

'I said that's not a problem. Alan?'

I am astonishingly grumpy. What is wrong with me?

I lurch into the toilets where I find a colleague, [Don't know his first name] Rogers, filling the kettle from the wash-basin. He insists it tastes better than the tap in the kitchen-ette (which does sometimes taste of chicken) but, speaking personally, it would have to taste a *lot* better for me to want to stand patiently by a tap while two yards away men are defecating.

'Are you OK?' he says, while human stools plop into a toilet bowl right next to his fresh water supply. 'Your mouth . . .'

I look in the mirror and see what he means. My mouth sports a bruise, which circles it completely like a purple flesh moat, while my lips appear stretched and a bit . . . baggy? The Maglite I'd held in my mouth really had been far too big for it, and I was in little doubt that this was the worst torch-related injury I'd had, perhaps ever. My poor, lovely mouth. The mouth that once suckled at my mother's teat(s), that first kissed Carol, that later kissed many other (better) kissers, that I used quite literally as a cakehole, that I used to utter the words that made me a comfortable living. It was staring back at me, slack and gaping and circled by a bruise in a grotesque parody of a ring road.

Well, this is the last thing I need. I'm brand ambassador for Corsodyl Mouthwash, for the whole of Anglia (not just East), and it's a contractual stipulation that I maintain a healthy mouth.[16] One look at this and they'll be well within their rights to stop my retainer and take back the pallets of Corsodyl they delivered to my garage.

My mouth looks and is very sore indeed, and I'm convinced it's misshapen. Why hasn't it sprung back? You'd expect it to spring back. The lips are stretched and ruddied, but when I attempt a smile, I stop and stare.

I'm looking at a familiar leer. It's the same leer I'd seen in the hand-hold of the cardboard box. And, now I think of it, the same leer my father used to do.

I feel something rise up inside me, like a phoenix, but a scaled-down one that fits into a tummy. It's as if the parallel I saw in that contused, slack smile had some . . . meaning.

Was there any meaning in this? That my mouth resembled the hand-hold of a cardboard box, which in turn resembled the grin of my long-deceased father? I had to know.

I returned to the studio and rushed through the rest of my show.[17]

***

I am sitting in front of the box in my loft. What could it contain?

I open it gingerly. Usually, I avoid opening boxes I don't

---

16 As well as 'tweet daily about mouths, mouthwash, gums, (fresh) breath and great taste of Corsodyl' and 'don't slag off Corsodyl'.

17 Although it ended at 2 p.m. regardless.

recognise – ever since a time looking for printer paper when I found what I thought was a brown paper bag of humbugs, only to discover they were dead wasps in a dormant nest. But did I realise that before eating one?[18]

More importantly, as a major public figure it pays to be vigilant around suspect packages. This comes from personal experience. When North Norfolk Digital was sent a box of heavy metal CDs,[19] muggins here was about to open it when fellow DJ Rudy Gibson shouted over, 'Careful, Alan. That contains anthrax.'

I hesitated, instantly and effortlessly aware that the spores of the bacterium *Bacillus anthracis* were used by bioterrorists in an increasingly common form of mail attack.

'Pardon?' I said. 'Can you repeat that please?'

'I said, careful, that contains *anthrax*.'

I looked at him, scarcely able to believe what he was suggesting. But he continued in more emphatic tones: 'The box of *heavy metal* CDs, Alan. Contains *anthrax*. You understand? Anthrax?'

He looked around, as if puzzled by my response. But I guess lesser guys would have panicked. Instead, I was centring myself. Stepping slowly away from the box and breathing in loudly and powerfully through my nostrils, before exhaling in short, fast bursts. Phuuuuuuuuuuuuuuuuuuur. Huh. Huh. Huh. Huh. Huh. Like that.

I ran to my car, pulling off my jumper and shirt, and then stood at my boot, slathering and rubbing my hands, face,

---

18 Yes, I did – which I appreciate makes the story a bit less interesting.

19 That's heavy-metal CDs. Rather than heavy, metal CDs!

chest and neck with handfuls of Swarfega while my colleagues watched from the upstairs windows, checking I was OK. Of course, I quickly realised Gibson had been joking and that Anthrax was the name of a heavy metal band or singer whose CD might have been in the box. I looked up at the window and waved and laughed and dressed and mused on how fantastic it was to have colleagues who could share practical jokes like this. Sure enough, I got into the spirit and played a practical joke on Gibson by getting my assistant to phone him during one of his shows to tell him his elderly mother had had a fall. He was all over the place!

But still, I think twice before opening strange packages.

Yet here I am, peering into the rectanguloid cardboard chamber (the box). I pull back the flaps, relieved to find neither dusty wasps nor anthrax, and see . . .

Oh my God, I don't believe it.

The box – the handle of which resembles the smile of my father, remember – contains bits and bobs that once belonged *to my father*. And here I am with baggy lips *that also resemble my father*, looking at the personal effects *of that father*. You have to admit that is a staggering coincidence. It's as if someone or some*thing* is trying to speak to me.

And there will be those who doubt that I'd stretched my lips in the first place, or who don't believe that a cutout handle looks anything like a mouth, or who, in any case, think this all feels 'conveniently neat'[20] or a 'confused mess'[21]

---

20 Eamonn Holmes.

21 My publisher.

or a 'blatant attempt to drum up poignancy'.[22] To those people I say, 'Are you calling me a liar?' And there'll be those who say, 'Yes, actually.' And to those people I say, 'Lawyer up.'[23] This actually happened. Why would I lie about it?

I look down at the box. I gulp loudly and like that [I've just stopped typing in order to click my fingers], I am transported back in time, spinning through space in front of a backdrop of calendars, alarm clocks and newspaper cuttings (or I would if this were a movie).

***

It's 20 February 1995. I am standing by a graveside, the wind whistling through my hair like a wind whistle. My father died on 15 February, and has now been buried. At a sparsely attended funeral, his casket has been blessed and lowered into the ground. I am invited to be the first to throw earth into the grave. I crouch down and, unsure of how much to put in (why don't they just tell you?), I push up my jacket sleeves and use both arms to sweep an enormous mound of earth from behind me and into the hole – like a couple of arm bulldozers. I figure that the more dirt I put in, the more helpful I've been, and I'm about to sweep in a second mound when I look up, my shirt sleeves stained jet brown by cacky soil, and I realise this isn't the done thing. My mother tuts and looks away.

My father has no savings to speak of. Mum tells me he didn't believe in savings, preferring instead to 'enjoy

---

22 My publisher.

23 Get a solicitor.

his money' by buying a new sofa every two years.[24]

I'm handed a box of his personal articles and put them in the car boot. And there they remain until I pay a younger, fitter man to pop them in my loft. And *there* they remain until now. I haven't looked inside because I find photographs of other people boring and receive enough mail of my own without wading through someone else's.

***

Back in my loft at Denton Abbey, I digest the contents of the box hungrily (although I don't eat them). But it contains little more than jottings, scribbled directions, a couple of letters, service-station receipts. I have to admit that my initial reaction is one of disappointment. It's all pretty meaningless, unless . . .? Wait a minute.

Seconds later, and I'm a blur of activity. It would work well as a montage sequence set to a piece of pop music.

I am sellotaping maps, letters, receipts and diary pages to the slanting walls of the loft. Then I'm fixing pieces of garden twine to connect relevant items together. I'm piecing together the movements and motives of a very particular incident in my father's life.

I stand by and assess my handiwork, struggling to see what it could all mean. But then I take a further step back, forgetting the roof space is now a lattice of twine, a 'cat scradle' stretching from one side to the other. I trip backwards into

---

24 He used to say, 'If you die owing money, you've beaten the system.' And when you think of that, you get a measure of the man.

it and am snared in the twine, like a naked man[25] trapped in the web of a giant information spider. And it's there, as I lie prone and chafing, that it all falls into place.

This box tells of a journey my father made. An important journey. A journey of hope to secure a better future for him and his family. A journey from Norwich to the nuclear power plant at Dungeness for a job interview.

It contains a cutout ad for an opening with British Nuclear Fuels Ltd at their power plant in Dungeness, plus a copy of a letter from my father, applying for a position at British Nuclear Fuels Ltd. My father had always been fascinated by science and the possibilities of nuclear fusion, albeit not enough to study it or anything. So when a position arose with BNFL, for my money the daddy of UK nuclear power, it stood to reason that he'd throw his hat into the ring.

The box also contains a letter from BNFL, inviting him for an interview. Plus a letter from him accepting the invitation. Plus a letter from BNFL confirming the date and time. Plus a letter from my father thanking them for their confirmation and confirming his confirmation, and asking them to confirm their receipt of his confirmation. Plus a letter from BNFL confirming receipt of my father's confirmation and informing him that thenceforth there was *no need for any further confirmation.*

The box also contains scribbled directions, showing that he had drafted three different routes from his home to the power plant before scribbling two out and circling the one he planned to take on the morning of his appointment. I

25 Forgot to say, I took my clothes off because I was hot.

smile. Chip off the old block, me! Although I have my assistant plot five routes and then I choose my favourite.

But the box also contains various receipts, for purchases of fuel and sandwiches (ten sandwiches)[26] from various points along the route.

But hang on, I think, still in my twine prison like a lo-tech piece of anti-gravity training. The timings don't add up. His purchases go on through not just the morning, but the whole day until the early hours of the next morning.

Also in the box is a letter from BNFL, expressing its regret that since my father had failed to attend the interview, his application would be taken no further. What happened? Why did he not show? What is the answer to this mysterious mystery?

And then I see it. There on the rejection letter are water marks, clear circles where liquid has dripped onto the parchment.[27] Could these be . . . the tears of my father? I fail to see what else could have caused them, positioned as they are in a dry box in a dry loft. Later, when I show the letter to my assistant – who by her own admission, or mine at least, can be a right snark – she brings up the fact that the roof had leaked the previous winter, but I know my father's tear marks when I see them. Does she honestly think she knows my father better than me?

And now that I think about it, I realise my father had never been the same after this day. I know because I remember.

---

26 My father loved sandwiches and would always chew a sandwich before eating a meal.

27 Well, paper.

Yes, this had truly been a pivotal moment for the Partridge Family.[28] Up until this point, Dad had been a wonderfully avuncular figure – certainly to me, since he spent most of his time with my cousins. He was a jovial chap who loved life and, as I say, sandwiches. After this point, I honestly don't think a sandwich ever passed his lips. He seemed greyer, sadder, hunched of shoulder and quick to temper. An absolute sod of a man, if I'm honest. Imagine the withering, acerbic put-downs of Rupert Everett directed at an eleven-year-old boy who's just trying to learn to ride a bike, and you'll have a sense of the man's entertaining nature.

He saw out his days in the job he'd held for years, at a dealership for Massey Ferguson, a US manufacturer of tractors and farming machinery, all of which were powered by diesel rather than controlled nuclear fusion – and remain so to this day. He became a hard man to be around and you'll remember, in my autobiography, I wrote some hard-hitting things about him that worked well in the tough-upbringing section. Could professional disappointment have been what made him so bitter, like it did with BT Sport's Ray Stubbs?

I wriggle free from the twine, my fall broken by a carpet of foil-backed polyurethane (seems the loft is insulated after all, but anyway . . .), and my eyes fill with tears like a big baby – because of the Dad thing, not because of the fall, or the insulation (although I am delighted about that).

It's the realisation that maybe, just maybe, I've judged my father too harshly. But now I've been gifted an insight into my father's life. A second chance to get to know him.

---

28 Not the TV show.

Suddenly, everything is clear. The reason for my restlessness, my listlessness, my zestlessness – the reason I am not at peace despite my living in a pretty eff-off house. There is a piece missing deep within me.

And now I know what I must do. I must complete the journey that my father never could. And I must do it on foot (can't remember why). It will be called the Footsteps of My Father Walk, and I must complete the Footsteps of My Father Walk to reach out, across the gap between this world and the next, to clasp my father's fingers and do right by him – to honour his memory and in doing so learn more about him and in doing so learn more about myself and in doing so create truly compelling copy.

'Alan!' I feel my name being whispered down the wind, as if his spirit is speaking with me. 'Alan! Alan! Alan!'

Then I realise it's my assistant shouting. She sounds panicky probably because I've ignored the doorbell. She's a ridiculous woman. Every time I don't answer the door because I'm towelling off or thinking or grumpy, she assumes the worst. Just because her former friend, a retired policeman, was found dead at home, she assumes we're all going to succumb to a stroke.

Her yelling continues until I answer the door to find her on her knees shouting through the letterbox, like a gynaecologist bellowing into a woman.

3.

SHIRT BACK ON NOW

***

'OK, ALAN, YOU CAN pop your shirt back on now.'

I'm with my GP, Dr Tony Bracegirdle, or 'Doc' as he's known on our pub quiz team, Cromwell's Bitches. He's a good friend and I've asked him to give me a full medical check-up, to ensure that it's safe to walk 160 miles in the Footsteps of My Father.

'What's the verdict, Doc?' I say to Doc.

He makes a few notes, in handwriting atypical of a GP. Most write in a lightning-fast but illegible scrawl. Doc, as befits a man who once spent ten hours in a John Lewis choosing a soundbar for his TV, writes slowly, clearly and deliberately, all while exhaling from his nose loudly. You should try being on a pub quiz team with him when you're meant to be handing your answer sheets in.

Eventually, he stops writing and turns to face me. 'Alan . . .'

He stops and takes off his glasses, to give his eyes a rub and enjoy another long, long nasal exhalation.

'Yes, Doc?'

'The thing is, Alan . . .'

He closes his eyes to consider how to word his answer and, yeah why not, enjoy another nasal exhalation. I stare at him impatiently. We're going to be late for the first round (TV theme tunes) and that's where the Bitches pick up most of our points.

Another nasal exhalation. I feel like sliding a harmonica onto the desk in front of him to see if he plays it remotely with his nose.

'Yes, Doc. Spit it out.'

'You're not a fit man, Alan. Your levels of physical fitness aren't what they should be. If you attempt this walk in your current physical condition, well, it's my medical opinion that . . .'

Another nasal exhalation.

'. . . you could seriously harm yourself.'

The news hits me like a clap (of thunder). I always thought I was in reasonable shape.

A retired headmistress I once briefly dated said I had the BMI and muscle definition of a man five-sixths my age. I'd stood up in my underpants to show off the results of a Sizzling Summer abs workout I'd read in the *Daily Mail*'s *Femail* magazine, and while my abdomen wasn't anything like a six-pack, I enjoyed being able to slap my belly without it making a loud clap. Standing there in the flickering light of a portable TV, letting the former educator look at my body and finish her cigarette, I pledged to remember how good it felt to be fit and strong, and promised myself I would develop a workout that would keep me in good shape for ever, and which I could pass on to others.[29]

But here I am, being told by Docky Bracegirdle that I'm a physical wreck. I need to do something, and fast. After all, I wasn't going to pull off a walk of this magnitude without first getting myself into quite superb physical condition, or 'QSPC' (my acronym).

I'd originally achieved QSPC as a teenager in the mid-1970s when I became one of the first children in Norfolk to take up an exciting avant-garde art form called 'Irish Dancing'. It's a dance of two distinct requirements, in which one's legs must move as quickly and violently as possible while one's arms and torso act as if they have no idea this is going on. And whether jigging with fellow dancers or practising alone in the abandoned quarry near my house, the pastime did wonders for my cardiovascular fitness. In short, it made my lungs absolutely massive, and being a big-lunged boy

---

29 I never got round to developing that workout. I got distracted trying to get a towbar fitted to my car for under £150, and forgot all about the day in Celine's bedroom. If you do want to get in shape though, try to find some old copies of *Femail* magazine because the Sizzling Summer abs workout was in there. It would have been around April or May 2011. Think it was *Femail* anyway. The gist of it was 'do lots of sit-ups'.

had all sorts of unexpected benefits. For a start, holding my breath became an absolute pleasure, and I'd often wow the girls by walking the entire way to school in just four gulps of air.

But it was when it came to whistling that QSPC was the real game-changer. Don't forget, this was a time when whistling *mattered*. Far from simply being the pastime of choice for grandads and postmen, in the 1970s everybody whistled. Even women. Whistling dominated the mainstream, but it also played an important role in our subculture. With a thriving underground scene – located primarily in my school – it's no exaggeration to say that whistling was the rap music of its day.

With my new-found pulmonary punching power, I could hold a note as long as your arm, if that's the phrase. And boy – or girl – did I make it count! Many was the time I'd reduce the playground to a reverential hush as I stood atop the climbing frame, head tossed back, hands miming a bugle, and whistled the entirety of the 'Last Post' in a single breath. It was a stunning achievement.

While I always appreciated the way my school colleagues would turn and stare, and I was always flattered by the celebratory hail of stones that would rain down on me at the end of a rendition, I could tell they didn't recognise the tune. And that troubled me. How could these children not even be on nodding terms with the basic musical staples of a military funeral? It's not as if they were toddlers. These people were nearly nine years old. What exactly *were* their parents teaching them at home? The mind boggles. Although this sorry tale may provide a clue as to why so many of my former classmates are now on zero-hour contracts.

***

Fast forward to the present day – got there yet? – and one thing I don't have is the luxury of time. Having spoken to my doctor, it isn't hard to read between the lines. Get into QSPC in the next two weeks or the walk to Dungeness will surely – *surely* – kill me. But is such a transformation even possible? Well, other than the fat back that's dogged me since the age of forty, I have a surprisingly toned body. Well proportioned and naturally hairless, it's a physique that's still able to draw admiring glances to this day, whether on a tropical beach or in the leisure-centre showers.

Of course, none of us are completely immune from the ravages of ageing. I'm not ashamed to admit that since 2010 my buttocks have become increasingly slack and gelatinous. Look at a photograph of my backside these days and it would bring to mind images of a cold bowl of porridge with a skin on the top. And I'm fine with that, not least because these photographs, taken at the start of each financial year, are purely for my own records.

The point I'm trying to make is this: while I may not be a meathead like Ben Fogle or Dan Snow, I do keep myself in pretty decent nick and see no need to spend my training time – as I know Dan does – trying to develop pecs 'as big as tits'.[30] No, my own training will focus on stamina, not strength.

***

Distance runners tend to train at high altitude. The thinner air is harder to breathe, which irritates them thus making them train harder. Many opt to base themselves in the highlands of Kenya, where, as well as some colossal altitudes, they're guaranteed a warm welcome from the Kenyish people.

For athletes enjoying a day off, there's also the chance to head out on safari, where with a fair wind and an experienced guide they might just come across the unforgettable sight of a rhino before it gets shot dead by an American

---

30 I'm reliably informed that Snow and Fogle, or 'Snogle', are a near-constant presence in the BBC gym, and that no one gets into the free weights area without their say-so. You can try it if you want, but the last presenter to do so got chased into the showers and savagely towel-whipped. Jeremy resigned from *Newsnight* the following day, his job prospects, not to mention his amateur clean-and-jerk career, in tatters.

In their tight Lycra shorts and matching white-leather weight-lifter's gloves, the powerfully nosed twosome push themselves to the limits. While one lifts, the other 'spots' his partner in Latin. '*Tempta vehementius!*' the spotter will bellow. '*Iterum!*' And as he pats his partner's muscles, he'll congratulate him on his work: '*Bene fecisti, bene fecisti . . .*'

But Snogle's true ire is reserved for those BBC presenters using the cardiovascular equipment. Nick Witchell, whose way of using the cross-trainer is admittedly *very* gay, gets more grief than most. Not that he minds. You can't be a royal correspondent who knows for a fact that the royals hate you without having a pretty thick hide.

tourist. I, myself, would never shoot big game (and would hesitate to even lay traps for them). You see, as a committed animal liker – *#animals* – I think very carefully about which animals I am and am not prepared to kill.

So as I say, something like a lion or an elephant is off the agenda. And my reason for that is probably the same as yours: if your bullets fail to kill these highly intelligent and increasingly endangered animals, you could be in real danger. Of course, other animals are to be found in greater numbers. Take pheasants. If anything, there are too many of them, and like most people who don't read the *Guardian*, I'd happily pick up a 12 bore shotgun to help control population numbers.[31]

Stamina training in Ethiopia is certainly an interesting idea, and one that I've come up with without any help, but as someone with a natural flair for geography – the capital of Azerbaijan is Baku – I know that combining my

---

31 Indeed, there's a growing school of thought – certainly among the National Hunt – that these well-liked game birds suffer from a rare form of avian depression, which means they don't want to live anyway. Worse still, animal rights campaigners have suppressed details of Sad Pheasant Syndrome because it goes against their blinkered desire to keep all animals alive, even if those animals don't wish to be alive.

Ask anyone who's ever seen a pheasant waddling around in a clearing, and they'll tell you the same thing – they just don't look happy. Shoulders slumped, beak down, it's all they can do to drag themselves from one god-awful second to the next. Definitive proof? Maybe not, and personally I'm reserving judgement, but surely there's cause for further investigation before the theory is shut down by the Linda McCartney brigade.

Norfolk-based radio show with daily trips to East Africa would be nigh-on impossible. Indeed, when I check it out with a local travel agent, I don't even mind that he sniggers at me because, as I say, I already know it's nigh-on impossible anyway. No, rather than feeling any anger towards this man, my main emotion is one of profound sadness.

In my experience, people who laugh at perfectly reasonable questions – enquiries about daily return flights from Norwich to Addis Ababa or otherwise – tend to be deeply insecure. My hunch is that, as a travel agent, he feels threatened by my far superior geography nous – Karachi has a population of 9.3 million – but was he right to pull that face and snort at me? Well, that's not for me to say. Instead, all I can do is report the facts and leave any such moral judgements to you, the reader.

And in that spirit, allow me to add a postscript. A few weeks ago, I had a verruca and was in town getting quotes from various chiropodists. I like to play chiropodists off against each other because I believe that my feet deserve the best care at the best possible price. I'll get a quote from three of them, then begin the mind games and negotiation that allow me – and my feet – to achieve a price we're comfortable with. The chiropodists don't like it, but knowing that I could easily opt for an over-the-counter alternative these days, they have little choice but to bend to my will.

(I should say at this point that I have decided to start referring to the travel agent by his name. My concern is that overusing the word 'he' is going to have a detrimental effect on my prose style and at the end of the day that has to take precedence over his right to anonymity.)

Grady Travel, owned by Elliott Grady, is located roughly halfway between two of Norwich's more price-malleable chiropodists. And as I walked past it that day, I noted that it was closed for lunch. Alas, the truth was far sadder. Grady's business had been liquidised, the victim of intense competition from the internet. Or so he says. Because while I don't have a dog in this particular fight, it does occur to me that if the internet is really such a threat to high-street travel agents then we'd all buy our holidays online, when of course we don't.

For his own sake – like I say, it doesn't affect me either way – I really hope that one day he can summon up the balls to admit to himself that his business actually failed because of his own haughty attitude towards customers, whether they were wanting to fly to Addis Ababa or otherwise. But even if he can't, I'm comforted to think that in his new job as a shelf stacker at Asda, Grady has at last found a role that – if he's honest – is better suited to his skills and abilities. And with shoppers asking him the location of everything from self-raising flour to gluten-free burgers, there's even a bit of geography thrown in for good measure (but at a level Grady can actually handle). And while that may sound trivial, it's the kind of knowledge that can bestow a certain dignity on a man, even if he is a shadow of his former self.

As for me, I need another plan. How will I get into QSPC?[32]

***

32 That question's aimed at you, by the way. I already know the answer.

WALLOP! A man's body smashes into the water, a billion tiny air bubbles fizzing around it like a nagging ex-wife.

PING! The lids of his eyes pop open but the balls of his eyes (his eyeballs) make a shocking discovery. Why the <u>hell</u> *is he naked?*

THE PAIN! Suddenly he's clawing at his peepers. Well, of course he is. <u>There's acid in the water.</u>

And stop.
Take a breath.
And another.
One more.
Good.

What you've just been experiencing is massive hit of pure adrenaline, brought on by a writing style so immediate, it was as if I were mainlining the images into your cerebral cortex with a big literary needle.

I adopted the style for good reason. Research shows that a lot of my readers went to polytechnics, which means reading for long periods of time can be incredibly challenging for them. I switched into a powerful, high-octane prose style, reminiscent of the early work of Lee Child, as a way of recapturing their attention.

Let's discuss it some more. You'll all have your own ideas as to what the story was about. Who was this mysterious person? And into what had he been plunged? Perhaps you had visions of a burly Eastern European gangster, stripped naked and shoved into an acid bath. Or a captured US serviceman, stripped naked and shoved into an acid bath. Or maybe you think he's a bent copper, shoved into an acid bath. Also naked.

Well, whichever you imagined, you'd be wrong. For a start, the acid bath – the one component common to all your ideas – doesn't even exist. Because while the principal character did believe there was acid in the water, there was no suggestion that he was in a bathtub.

No, in actual fact what I was describing was nothing more sinister than a trip to the local swimming pool. The passage told the story of a man (Alan Partridge, or me) diving in and feeling the perfectly innocent sting of chlorine in his/my eyes.[33] An essentially mundane activity has now been seared onto your mind's eye, all through the power of words.

Let's carry on.

WHOOSH! He's swimming now, his body slicing through the water like a sharp dolphin.

SWELL! The effort of swimming, combined with a healthy diet, is making his muscles develop right here in the pool!

TUMBLE TURN! He attempts a tumble turn.

PLTHWAH! He emerges from the tumble turn and coughs chlorine-filled water off to the side.

PEEP! The lifeguard blows his whistle. 'Hey, quit speeding!' he shouts through the whistle.

---

33 The suggestion of nakedness is, I concede, harder to explain. Unlike certain adult-only swimming pools in Germany and Scotland, bathing without trunks is prohibited in England. And I for one take great care to ensure I always wear mine. No, I was using something called 'artistic licence', which is a literary term for lying. For authors such as myself it can be a real boon, allowing us to make up anything we want and never be challenged on it.

And stop.

Breathe.

OK, good.

The tang in the back of your throat, the pounding head-ache? Adrenaline again. Rest a while. It will pass.

We could carry on in this vein indefinitely, but it's tiring for you to read and exhausting for me to write. The point is, when your publisher tells you to skip the training section because it only works on film and is boring in prose, it's not hard to make them eat those words and prove once and for all that they don't know what they're on about and should maybe pipe down in future.

So why am I in a swimming pool? Well, I don't like walk-ing because walking is boring and also I have two cars. And while I am well aware that walking will be hard to avoid once I set off on the Footsteps of My Father Walk, that doesn't mean it has to feature in my training. Instead, I have decided to build up stamina by swimming.

'Swimming' is an ancient technique in which the co-ordinated thrashing of the arms and legs provides propul-sion through water. Effectively, the human participant briefly becomes a boat. Well suited to those with large shoulders and feet like spades, swimming enjoyed a boost in popular-ity in Victorian times when, due to advancements in water husbandry, we were able to domesticate H_2O, trapping large amounts of it in four-sided pits or 'pools'.

I myself have been swimming since early childhood, and while I wouldn't describe myself as a 'water baby' (the word 'baby' suggests weakness), I've certainly had a life rich in aquatic activity. True, I didn't enter a swimming pool at all between the ages of six and eleven because I became scared of an imaginary water monster called Quaddy, but, as I say, other than that, I'm certainly no stranger to the way of the Speedo.

Historically, my technique of choice was the backstroke. It's a tricky one to master because you can't really see where you're going, but as a young man I always had more than enough spatial awareness to avoid any WTAs (water traffic accidents). Of course, as you get older, keeping your bearings becomes increasingly difficult, which is why recently, with incidences of me crashing on the rise, I took the difficult decision to retire the backstroke in favour of its far safer cousin, the breaststroke.

Training-wise, my plan is to swim each morning at 6 a.m., although on day two I switch to 7 a.m. because I discover that the leisure centre doesn't open until 7. The key thing is to rack up miles. I estimate that if I can swim for two hours each day it will give me a fighting chance of avoiding the near-certain death that my doctor so clearly implied awaited me on the road.

Pretty soon I settle into a routine. With my alarm set for 5, I hit snooze every ten minutes until just before 7, at which point it's time to start the day. With no need for a shower – the swim will get me clean – I can be out of the house in minutes. To get me in the right frame of mind, the drive to the leisure centre is soundtracked by a mega-super-maxi-mix of nautical theme tunes – *Blue Peter*, *Das Boot*, *Howards' Way*, not to mention the music from *Jaws*. Yes, the image of a Great White somehow finding its way into Norwich Leisure Centre's municipal pool and causing pandemonium

– and it *would* be pandemonium – never fails to raise a smile.

For breakfast? Well, it's all about the protein. In the car I have two hard-boiled eggs washed down with a one-litre protein shake (which I think might also be made from eggs).[34,35]

Into the changing rooms and the process of getting ready is a cinch because all I have to do is remove my coat and pyjamas. I don't even have to put my trunks on. Fearful of forgetting them due to morning grogginess, I always make sure to put them on before I go to bed. It's an elegant solution.

I have to confess that the swimming itself is harder. Two hours is a long time to sustain constant physical activity, and in the first few days I often find myself asleep in the water. I realise I have to slow my pace. What that means, however, is that I end up being lapped by another early morning swimmer, a pensioner who calls herself Dawn and indeed is called Dawn. Now, in and of itself, being overtaken by a retired dinner lady isn't a problem. Whereas Dawn is here to keep fit (or as fit as a pensioner can realistically be), I am in training for a challenging endurance event in the footsteps of my father.

Of course, her attitude towards me shouldn't matter. But it does. Big-style. She clearly thinks my slow and steady pace is the fastest I can swim. And although she never says that to me, she doesn't have to. The patronising 'Morning' as she swims past me. The irony-laden 'Enjoy the rest of your swim'

---

34 Yep, it is. I checked the label. Ingredients: eggs, water.

35 Incidentally, if you're ever on this kind of diet, remember to eat some roughage. 'All protein and no fibre makes Alan a blocked boy.'

as she climbs out to get changed. No, that woman's feelings could not be clearer. And something needs to be done.

As I sit in front of the TV angrily eating crisps, it comes to me. I will challenge her to a race. Yes, the more I think about this idea, the more I like it, and the more I find myself nodding in appreciation. The idea brings to mind the duels of days gone by, and also other events from the past where, rather than being team-based, it was just one person against one other person.

Oh, how sweet my victory will be. I can almost taste it now – salty, perhaps even slightly meaty, although that may just be the crisps. The race will be two lengths of the pool and I will beat her comfortably; ripping her, to use a piece of modern-day parlance that personally I find deeply unpleasant, a new arsehole.

Yet the next morning, 'Dawn' doesn't show. Nor the next morning. Nor the next. With the days running out until I have to head off in the footsteps of my father, I begin to lose hope.

And then, on my final morning in the pool, out of the blue (literally, in this case – the women's changing rooms had recently been painted aqua), 'Dawn' appears. It seems the gods are smiling down on me, perhaps from a large cloud high in the stratosphere, or maybe from up in the swimming pool's viewing gallery (where they can enjoy a cup or two of the sublime 'chicken-flavoured soup drink' dispensed from its vending machine).

But back to 'Dawn'.

'Morning,' she calls over as I breaststroke through the water.

'Yeah, whatever,' I think back at her.

'Morning,' she says again.

'Yes, I heard you the first time,' I reply, still inside my head. 'I wanna race you,' I add, but this time outside my head.

With the gauntlet laid down, I allow myself to sink away under the water. It's a powerfully dramatic exit. It isn't even a problem that I'm in the shallow end and am only inches below the surface. I just tuck my knees into my chest and go into the mushroom position until I'm sure she's gone.

But there's a problem. While under the water, I begin to play back the incident that has just unfolded. I realise Dawn didn't hear what I said. My words were obscured by a loud splash. In clear contravention of the International Code of Conduct for Swimming Baths, a teenager had entered the pool by performing a bomb.

Knowing that action needs to be taken, I quickly and efficiently de-mushroom, my head popping back up above the water like some sort of benevolent human kraken. The lifeguard hasn't taken any action against the naughty boy, so like any right-minded person, I attempt to catch his eye and tut. But my mouth, still sodden from all the swimming I've been doing, is simply too wet. And instead of tuts, the best I can muster is a series of squelching noises that make it sound like I'm eating, ironically another act expressly prohibited by the international code.

Worse, when I look back, Dawn has gone and is heading back into the changing rooms, having forgotten her distinctive yellow nose clip. These clips, perched at the end of a user's nose, force the outside walls of the nostrils flush against the septum, creating a water-tight seal. Yet though we understand a great deal about the mechanics of such clips, the reasons why female pensioners insist on wearing them are less well understood. Some have suggested that as women age, an abnormality in the X chromosome means they forget they're not supposed to sniff underwater. Others are more cynical, believing that elderly women wear them because they think that having a deeper, more nasal tone of voice makes them more attractive to lifeguards, many of whom are less than a quarter of their age. Not that any of this is my concern. All I want to do is race the bloody woman. I shall stand outside the changing rooms and wait.

Nine minutes later, I'm still waiting. What *is* she doing in there? It doesn't take nine minutes to find a nose clip. Certainly not a distinctive yellow one. Besides, hovering by the entrance to the women's changing rooms looks weird, especially for a middle-aged broadcaster in the current climate.

I slide back into the pool, creating barely a ripple.[36] I've decided to keep swimming, aware – perhaps even 'keenly' aware – that I still have a few minutes of my daily two-hour session to complete. Slow and steady, I glide through the water. Yes, it's at times like these that I think I'd be quite content to have been born a merman (though ideally one furnished with a set of fully functioning genitals). But all this daydreaming about being a merman, and about falling in love with a mermaid who looks quite a lot like Daryl Hannah in *Splash*, only with brown hair, means I've failed to notice

---

36 Of all the disciplines involved in swimming, I am perhaps most adept at the getting in.

Dawn. She's back in the pool – nose-clip clamped onto her nostrils – and is about to begin her swim.

I need to get down to her end, and fast. Clearly this is a moment tailor-made for the front crawl, but I can't do front crawl so instead I opt to skull, the swan-like grace of my upper body belying the fact that under the water my legs are going absolutely gangbusters. Within seconds I reach the shallow end, where I allow myself to become beached. I swivel my head Dawn-wards.

'Morning,' she says.

'That's original,' I think.

'Having a nice swim?' This woman is unbelievable, it's all I can do not to flick water at her. It's time for me to do some of my own out-loud speaking. I fire up my vocal chords.

'You and me. It's on.'

'What's that, love?'

But I'm not ready to answer yet. I'm too busy slowly nodding my head while mouthing the words 'It's on. It's on.'

Dawn swims off down the pool without even responding. Oh, this woman is a real piece of work. No matter, I'll soon rein her in. I stand up, chlorinated water cascading off my glistening body, my giant frame casting a shadow across the majority of the shallow end. Raising my arms above my head, my fingers pointing upwards, my thumbs touching, I execute a textbook standing dive. Within moments I've caught her up.

'Having a nice swim?' I say as I burn past her.

'Yes, thank you,' she replies, pretending she doesn't realise I'm shoving her own words back down her throat.

Within a minute I've lapped her – God, that was easy

– but then: disaster. As she stops to chat to a friend (the nerve of the woman) I get into difficulty in the deep end. In my determination to best Dawn I've forgotten that I've only just finished a gruelling two-hour swim. I am also dangerously low on calories, having forgotten to drink my egg smoothie that morning. And now, with victory in sight, cramp has struck. With spasms ripping through my muscles, and with the lifeguard busy sending a text, I know I am in trouble. I begin to sink.

Then, a saviour. Hooking an arm around my neck and swimming me ashore (i.e. to the side of the pool) is none other than Dawn. To some, this would be the ultimate humiliation. Not only have I failed to finish the race but I've had to be rescued by my geriatric nemesis. Clearly, though, that is the wrong way to look at things and you'd have to be quite thick to do so. The reality is that by zooming past Dawn and extending that lead to over a length, I have proved myself the superior swimmer, thereby exacting my revenge for two weeks of sneering condescension from the narcissistic seventy-year-old. Never again will she mock me; never again will she imagine, even in her wildest dreams, that she could come close to the kind of pace and power of which I am so clearly capable.

That said, I would like to thank Dawn for saving my life.

4.

BE PREPARED

***

I'M SKULKING NEAR A BAR in a media haunt called the Hospital Club in central London. It's the wrap party for series thirty-eight of *Watchdog*, the BBC consumer rights show, which I still think should have been called *Ombudsman*. But tonight, I'm keeping my opinions on that to myself. I have a job to do.

I've managed to blag the 'plus one' of *BBC Breakfast*'s Bill Turnbull. His wife isn't happy about being bumped – she'd had her hair done and everything – but Bill knows he owes me one after I agreed to provide his urine sample when bosses sprung a surprise medical on the team. He's across the room, glowering in that way of his. Bill, cheer up. We're even.

I sip at a mineral water and lurk around, my eyes literally

peeled for a certain someone. And then I spot my prey. Pay dirt! I zoom across the room, on fast legs, and extend my hand. 'Harvey!'

It's Harvey Kennedy, the agent I'd met outside the Langham and the man behind some of broadcasting's most high-profile walkers.

'Well, this is a surprise,' I say, shaking his hand warmly.[37] It's not a surprise. I knew he'd be here. After a bit of digging, I managed to get my hands on his client list and discovered he represented *Watchdog* presenter Matt Allwright, a broadcaster I've got a lot of time for (and whose surname is probably about fair. I think Matt Excellent or even Matt Verygood would be pushing it, but as I say – lot of time for the chap).

'This your wife?' I say, referring to the younger lady on whose small-of-back Harvey's hand is resting. They both smile with their mouths and he gradually removes his hand and lets her walk ahead.

'It's Alan,' I remind him. 'Alan Partridge. Mind if I run something by you?'

And I tell him all about the Footsteps of My Father Walk, and about how excited people have got when I've told them about it. It's a walk, I tell him, *dripping* with emotional and historical significance which takes in some of the most tele-visual parts of east England. HD telly was made for this. Eventually, I finish and waggle my hands as if to say, 'Ta-da!'

'Great,' he says. 'Really great.' And he looks far over my shoulder as if visualising a lucrative and mutually successful future.

---

37 I have very warm hands.

I look at him, nodding.

'Yes,' he continues. 'You should definitely do it.'

'And you think broadcasters will be keen?' I ask.

'Why not,' he smiles. 'Why not. Yes, I can definitely . . . see that.'

'You can see that can you, Harvey?' I say.

'Yes,' he says. 'Definitely.'

I give him a full rundown of the itinerary. He gives me a thumbs up, which I don't mind saying is one of the greatest thumbs up *this* Partridge has ever received.

'Well, I'll leave that with you!' I shout after him. 'Letcha do ya thang with the commissioners! And tell them I want my name in the title or I'll . . .'

But at that moment a waiter bearing blinis[38] cuts between us and I'm distracted. I grab fifteen or so, piling them onto a napkin like it's the last lifeboat off the *Titanic*, and by the time I allow the boy to walk on, Harvey has disappeared into the crowd. Curses! Foiled by my own rumbling tummy, just as we were about to shake on the deal.

I have my assistant call his office the next morning, but he's not in. Perhaps he's pitching the idea to commissioners. I don't know. I can always call back. It's fine.

***

Early start today so I could pop to Prontaprint and get fresh business cards printed. These are exactly the same as the old ones but they have 'As Seen on TV' in a star in the top-right corner. The star obscures the picture of the partridge I had

---

38 Minuscule pizzas.

in that corner, so it looks like the head of the hapless bird is exploding, but I don't mind that because . . . well, my head *is* exploding. I'm Billy Big Head![39]

My assistant argues that pride is sinful but she's not been off terrestrial telly for two decades. So, very much against her wishes, I have her sit in the passenger seat of my car while I drive to visit a few choice friends who live in the area.

First stop is Formula One commentator Martin Brundle, who's famous for being catty when it comes to other people's careers. I pull up outside his house and beep the horn. 'Oh, Martiiiiiiin!' I sing-song until he comes to the front door. 'Guess who's back in the big tiiiiiime?' That's my assistant's signal to throw one of my new business cards onto his lawn while I put my foot to the floor and zoom away.

Next, it's former queen of daytime Trish Goddard. 'Oh, Triiiisha!' I sing until she comes to the front door. 'Guess who's back in the big time?'

'Fuck should I know?' she snaps. But as she speaks my assistant is tossing her a biz card and we are outta there!

Next stop is Jamie Theakston, the spiky-haired kiddies' TV presenter. 'Oh, Jaaaaaamie!' I sing. He doesn't come to the door for ages, even though I know he's in. Eventually, I pepper my singing with parps of the horn until he comes

---

39 To be clear, this is not a reference to William Gabitas, the son of my late friend. Although he is referred to as Billy Big Head in and around Norwich, in his case it's because he has an unusually huge head (an optical illusion caused by his thick, bushy hair, which fluffs up when he takes his motorbike helmet off in a hot pub). Whereas I'm Billy Big Head because I'm *feeling* bigheaded.

to the front window. 'Guess who's big in the back time?'

As I had fluffed my line very slightly, my assistant didn't throw the business card, so I grab it off her and throw it myself. It only gets as far as the pavement but I know this will frack Jamie off hugely.

Next stop is Delia Smith, the lightly mottled Norwich-based cook. 'Oh, Delia!' I sing-song. She's at the door in a flash. 'Guess who's back in the big time?'

My assistant tosses a business card, and I'm about to ske-daddle when I realise Delia's husband Michael [Smith?] has parked in front and boxed me in. Delia clasps her hands together and approaches the car as I rev the engine.

'Oh, Alan,' she says. 'That's wonderful!' And I remember Delia's always been lovely to me, as long as I clean my plate. She invites me in and we have a really nice cuppa, which I concede makes for a slightly anticlimactic end to my day of drive-by and means I don't have time to stop at Neil Buchanan's flat or Michaela Strachan's commune.

Still, a delightful morning. And then it's off to work.

***

Of course, the training and new-business-card printing will all be pointless if my bosses at North Norfolk Digital don't agree to give me the time off. It's a matter I know I have to handle with gloves made from the skin of a baby goat.[40]

---

40 Another consequence of Yewtree: the North Norfolk Digital legal team recently advised that on-air staff should refrain from using the phrase 'kid gloves' in case people took it to be an inappropriate refer-ence to mittens.

Unlike factory workers, cabbies or teachers, radio DJs can't just take ten days off whenever the feeling takes them. I happen to have enormous respect for all of those professions, but – and I think they'd agree with this – one factory worker or cabbie or teacher is much the same as any other.

Take the teachers. No one's ever heard of a pupil turning up to class to find there isn't a teacher there. Instead, if the rostered educator is absent, another one simply takes his or her place, with no harm done to academic standards. Hard-working and valuable as they are, you'd never hear anyone say they remembered a specific, say, English teacher. All they'd remember is that they were *taught* English. But with DJs it's different.

Rightly or wrongly (by which I mean 'wrongly'), people feel they have a direct relationship with DJs. We're like their friends, albeit friends who keep breaking off the conversation to play a record or throw to the weather.

When it comes to listener figures, breakfast shows are king. At North Norfolk Digital we have the peerless Beverley Bacton. As the anchor of the seven-till-nine slot, Beverley enjoys a higher profile, a larger pay packet and – tougher to justify – a better parking space than any other DJ. With her cancer scare now long behind her, Bev is a confident and vocal presence around the station. And with so many people demanding her attention, it's no surprise she can rarely find the time to put her dirty mugs in the dishwasher like everyone else.

Yet the listeners' connection with breakfast-show DJs is an interesting one. A breakfast show is something that tends to be on anyway. You're chomping on some cereal, you're ironing your tie, you're brushing your hair into the perfect side-parting. You might as well listen to something, right? So you bung on the breakfast show and it's fine, it's absolutely fine.

Ditto the other plum slot in the schedules – drivetime. You've had a tough day, your boss is a git, your breath stinks because you're so hungry, the last thing you're going to do is struggle through rush-hour traffic in total silence. What you need is something untaxing to take your mind off things – something that won't challenge you or require you to think in any way whatsoever. So what do you do? You flick on a drivetime show. Great. Perfect. Job done.

But consider another type of radio programme. Consider, for the sake of argument, my own slot, mid-morning. People are busy in the mid-morning. The high-powered executive isn't just listening to a radio show 'because it's on'. For a start, it's not on. Why would it be? He's got a conference call with Peking in five minutes and if he doesn't close the deal with Wangzu Plastics, his entire UK workforce will be in jeopardy. Or whatever.

The same goes for other types of employee. Sorry for swearing, but they've got 'shit' to do. The point is, if you listen to mid-morning radio it's because you want to; it's because a certain DJ connects with you, often in a way you haven't experienced since the death of your late husband. That's why mid-morning DJs tend to have the strongest bond with their listeners. So if that kind of figure disappears from the schedules for a period of, what, two weeks, there are gonna be problems.

What form these problems might take is a different matter. A lot of damaged people listen to my show (at the last count there were over 3,000) and, while I love them dearly, guessing how they're going to react to any given situation is a fool's errand. So it's no great surprise when my written request for time off is met with a swift rejection by station manager Greg Frampton. I decide to pay him a visit.

'Ding, dong!' I used to love doing that thing where you *say* 'knock, knock' instead of actually *doing* a knock. But now that other people have started copying me I've been forced to innovate. These days I prefer to make the sound of a doorbell. Admittedly, internal doors don't have doorbells, but any concerns over accuracy are easily overridden by the sheer freshness of the idea.

'Oh hello, Alan.'

Greg is looking up from a pasty he's bought, with a disappointing lack of imagination, from Greggs. Time for me to go in for the kill.

'I need that time off, buddy.'

Greg's Greggs pasty now lies prone on his desk. And I'll be honest, it stinks.

'You can't have the time off.'

'Look, I know this isn't easy for you. You're worried about our sponsors. But trust me, United Farm & Animal Feed aren't going anywhere. I paintball with their MD. He wouldn't dare to pull out. He's chicken shit. Which they put in the feed apparently.'

'Alan, I'm not worried about the sponsors.'

'The listeners, then. Which again, I totally get. A lot of

them are in care homes and get me piped in. Remove Alan Partridge from their daily equation and all they have left is meals.'

'Alan, it's none of that. You just haven't got the leave.'

By this point he's looking shifty and makes a hasty exit. He claims he has a meeting to go to, even though both he and I know he's just going to stand in the bogs for ten minutes. I like Greg and am very fond of his wife and young family, but that doesn't stop him being a truly spineless human being. Sometimes I don't know how he even stands up, let alone goes to Pilates (which I know for a fact he does).

I'll spare you the details, but what follows is a week of tense negotiation via both email and shouting. I restate my desire to follow in the footsteps of my father, the station restates its desire to refuse, I threaten to call in the union, the station says that's my prerogative. I remember that I'm not a member of a union and I hate unions. Finally, though, at the eleventh hour (or rather, the fourteenth hour, it's 2 p.m.), an acrimonious compromise is hammered out. To wit, I am permitted to take the time off, but can do so only as unpaid leave and on the condition that I stop leaving so many ideas in the company suggestion box.

I agree, and to show there are no hard feelings, I reply to Greg's final email with a series of positive emoticons: thumbs-up, applauding hands, bicep flex, 'perfect' sign, jug of beer, galloping horse, high-heeled shoe.

***

'G-g-g-g-good morning, l-l-l-l-listeners.' WTF? I sound like some sort of polite machine gun. I'm about to share the news of my impending time off and haven't been this nervous since the final day of the 02–03 tax year, when I'd had a bad few months and came perilously close to not being able to say I was a higher-rate taxpayer. I quickly slap on a track and turn to my on-air sidekick Simon Denton, aka 'Sidekick Simon'.

'I need to clear my head.'

'That shouldn't take long.'

It really is incessant with this guy. We're not even on air. I can only assume his parents neglected him as a child and he's now stuck in an endless cycle of trying to win people's approval. Either that or he's just so simple he genuinely doesn't know when he is and isn't on air. To be honest, both seem plausible.

'I'd heading out for a minute. If I'm not back by the time this song finishes, would you mind filling in?'

Say whaaaat?! Simon's eyes light up. Like all sidekicks, he dreams of emerging from his master's shadow. Most red-blooded males fantasise about a busty woman soaping herself down in the shower; Simon fantasises about having his own radio show with me as his sidekick(!). And while I don't think his fantasies are sexual – although obviously I can't rule that out – they do exert a powerful hold over the former lab technician. And, as his boss, that's something I use to my advantage.

I pride myself on giving Simon plenty of honest feedback,

emailing him each evening at 11 with a full breakdown of his performance on that day's show. Much like Noel Edmonds, however, Simon has an incredibly thin skin. Always mindful of this, I make sure that for every ten items of constructive criticism, I provide at least one piece of praise – 'you arrived on time today'/'you remembered to use antiperspirant instead of deodorant'/'you sat quietly at the back while I interviewed the guest'.

Over time, however, these emails, so crucial to improving the quality of the show, grind his confidence to dust. That's why every couple of months or so I pull out the carrot of more airtime and dangle it in front of his not inconsiderable nose.

I've got a hell of a lot of time for Simon Denton and genuinely believe that his ability to think up a pun at short notice puts him right up there with the very best of the Cambridge Footlights guys, and not a million miles behind the people who write Christmas cracker jokes. But being a DJ requires different skills. Not only does Simon not have these skills, he doesn't know what they are. I like people with ambition, and wanting more airtime is a fine goal for him to have. Interestingly, though – and I'm only saying this because I care about him – it might actually be more helpful to Simon if we reduced his airtime. Maybe then he'd be able to relax and start finding his feet, perhaps even managing to cut out that wheezy breathing he does when he's worried a joke hasn't gone down well.

So while he'll most likely never get the extra airtime he craves – in this case I've put on the whole of Queen's seminal album *Jazz*[41] so will easily be back before it finishes – that's not the point. The point is that techniques such as 'cover for me if I'm not back in time' make him think he has potential. And that's more than enough to restore his motivation until the next time. Call it good management, call it being a friend, it just works.

With Simon's mood much improved, I am able to attend to my own issues. My nerves need quashing. Thankfully, I know exactly what to do, and head to the disabled toilet to centre myself with some mindfulness techniques and half a bottle of white wine.

As it transpires, I needn't have worried. The reaction of my listeners – to borrow an image from the world of stamps – is absolutely 'first class'. No sooner do details of my planned journey plop from my mouth and into the black foamy head of the North Norfolk Digital microphone, than listeners begin to contact the show in their droves. I don't know how many people get in touch with messages of support that morning, but suffice to say I lose count at nine. 'Good luck, Alan. Take as long as you need.' 'Don't hurry back, Alan.' 'Will Wally Banter be filling in? He's great.'

I am deeply touched.

---

41 Notable for the song 'Fat Bottomed Girls', which mocks the larger-backsided lady. I once bumped into Brian May at Jodrell Bank and pointed out that women were *meant* to have fatter bottoms than men: as well as being an evolutionary trait to attract a mate, women have higher oestrogen levels, which deposit fat around the buttocks and thighs. Indeed, there's evidence that a larger bottom reduces the risk of osteoporosis and angina. We've been friends ever since.

***

At 2 p.m. I stride into the kitchenette and enjoy my post-show pint of water. Greg walks by and I glower at him. Fellow d-jock Bev Bacton watches me and I explain to her that Greg would do well to show me a bit more respect – as would everyone. And that I've a good mind to sack this job off entirely and focus on my TV work.

'What TV work?' she asks, and I slide her one of my business cards without even looking. It's a cool move and no mistake.

She's confused, so I explain about the Footsteps of My Father Walk and the likelihood of it becoming a six-part TV series. She frowns and says, 'Well, if it's a done deal . . .'

I expected that kind of sniffiness. Around the station, the reactions of my colleagues and enemies are just as muted. When a man steps outside his comfort zone, when he dares to imagine the unimaginable, when he decides to walk from Norwich to Dungeness in the footsteps of his father, it captures people's imagination/s.

But it also provokes darker feelings. Ever heard of 'the green-eyed monster'? Yes, a few nods of recognition there. Well, for those of you who haven't, it's a phrase, presumably stemming from a Disney film, that refers to someone who's jealous. And there are plenty of those, although some have good reason. Friend and voiceover artiste John Meber would love to walk anywhere, let alone to Dungeness, but a recent car crash – for which I'm afraid John was entirely to blame – has put paid to his spine. John now lives in a wheelchair.

As for the rest of them, their envy is born out of simple self-hatred. To even attempt a walk of this scale, you need seriously big balls. Thankfully for me, I've got a pair of 'em. Although it's funny, because if my actual ones were the size of my metaphorical ones, I wouldn't even be able to stand up, let alone walk. Effectively stranded on top of a couple of giant hairy beanbags, I'd have to see out my days in a care home for the clinically big-balled.

But my colleagues don't have my kind of bravery and they know it. They're small people with small lives and small dreams, and even though a guy from accounts keeps telling me that he does triathlons, the overall length of most triathlons is about thirty miles. I'm walking over five times that distance, which means my walk is over five times harder than one of his triathlons, and I think any reasonable person would agree with that.

Yet whatever I hear these people mumble about me as I pass them in the corridor – and the term 'sad prick' seems to be the most popular – I'm not about to hold a grudge. In fact – and I'm going to surprise you here – I actually forgive them.

When I was young – i.e. up to the age of fifty – almost all of my actions were motivated by revenge. If you had wronged me, then sooner or later you'd have it coming to you. It might not be that week, it might not be that year, but if your name was on the list I kept in a Harrogate Toffee box buried in my garden, then trust me, the die had been cast. And while I have to admit that some of the happiest times of my life have been as a result of getting someone back, the quest for retribution was an exhausting one.

Let's say a colleague has caused offence by failing to compliment you on your new haircut. It's not like they haven't noticed. It's shorter than before, it's got gel in and the way the fringe flops over to the right makes you look, what, five years younger? Yet they don't say a word. Where's the best place to pay them back? Think about it for a moment. You know for a fact they'll be at work every day, you even know where their desk is. But that would be too easy, too obvious, even. Better by far to do it where they feel safest: their home. Order sixty Littlewoods catalogues to be delivered to the place where they live, where their partner lives, where their *children* live, and you can seriously shake them up.

But it also takes time. You can flirt with Helen in HR all you want, but by law she's not allowed to give out employee addresses. Plus, you'll then need to deal with the fallout when she gets the wrong end of the stick and invites you to go ten-pin bowling with her. No, the only way to get this done is to go old school. Tailing the person as they leave work, you figure out where they live. From there, it'll be four or five nights parked over the road. How many people live there? What are their comings and goings? Do they have a pet that can be kidnapped? Is there a rockery that can be trashed?

Surveillance isn't easy, though. You'll need warm clothes, a camera with telephoto lens, two Thermos flasks (one for tea, t'other for wee) and *for God's sake remember your sandwiches*.

With your research dossier now complete, it's time to make a plan. Head into your garage to start brainstorming ideas on a large whiteboard purchased from a local school. Start by scribbling down any idea that comes into your head. Most will be criminal offences but don't worry about that for now. Cross out only those that are genuinely disturbing, otherwise relax, let the ideas flow and *for God's sake remember your sandwiches.*

These days, however, I see the world a little differently. My longing for revenge, much like the foreskin of an adult Jew, simply isn't there any more. Sure, hidden in a bush at the end of Bruno Brookes's drive last week, I was still convulsed with spasms of ecstasy on seeing him open his front door, only to be greeted by a pizza he hadn't even ordered, but otherwise I'm a changed man.

And if that thirst for besting those who have wronged me does return at any stage during my walk, then that's fine too. Because needless to say, I'll have the last laugh.

***

'Well, if it's a done deal . . .'

The words of Beverley Bacton in the kitchenette haven't bothered me but they have stayed with me. She's a cautious woman, as evidenced by the prenup she makes her husbands sign, but maybe there's something in that.

Just to get things solidified, I reach out to Harvey Kennedy again. I manage to get my assistant to call his office and patch me through, a concept that takes around an hour of explaining before she grasps it.

'Harvey,' I say when I speak to him. 'Just calling to see if we got that commission? Are you well?'

'Indeed.'

I punch the air. Then something occurs to me. 'Are you answering the first question or the second question?'

Silence.

'Or did that answer apply to both questions? Harvey. Harvey, mate. Harvey?'

'I think I pressed something.' This is my assistant's voice and in despair I look heavenwards, even though I don't believe in it and she does. I sigh and fire off an email.

'Harvey. When you said "indeed", were you answering the first question (did we get a commission?) or the second question (are you well?)? Or did that answer apply to both questions? Please advise.'

I spend the rest of the day checking my emails but he must be out-of-office because I hear nothing back. It's fine, though, because like I say, it's not really about getting a TV series. It's about honouring Dad. I can't emphasise that enough.

5.

MORE THAN MY FAIR SHARE

***

THE QUESTION I'VE BEEN ASKED more than any other is this: is the walk for charity? Honestly! If I had a pound for every person who asked me that, I'd give it to charity, of course. But the walk itself must *not* be for charity, I was certain of that.

It's not a decision I have taken lightly. I am a *huge* fan of charity and even had direct debits set up at one point[42] before my online banking started to look cluttered and I had a purge. Indeed, I hope that before long our collective donations will do so much for the needy that the Exchequer

---

42 Help for Heroes, Friends of John Meber and Eton College.

can do away with income tax, the mandatory 'charitable donation' that everyone seems to be fine with, perhaps because they haven't bothered to think it through.

No, I'm bang into charity, all right. I've done sponsored swims, sponsored shaves and even popped my head and hands in medieval stocks so that, for a pound a pop, church fete attendees could throw wet sponges at me, similar to the very Old Testament stonings that Jesus supposedly got rid of when he rebranded God as a nice chap. Indeed, I'm sure the Messiah would have had something to say about the older lads – still Christians, remember – loading up sponges with hot coffee and wanging them full pelt at my frightened face.

One year, I even got involved in North Norfolk Digital sales team's charity 'dress down Friday'. Unlike the creative side of the operation, our advertising lot are required to wear shirts, ties and suits (don't know why). Well, when muggins here heard that they were permitted to wear their casual clothes in exchange for a £5 donation, he/I couldn't help but get involved. Except I had to invert the idea, because of course on a normal day I get to wear what I want.

Well, picture their *faces* when Partridge strolls in, pops £5 in the collection box and says, 'Morning.' The sales floor looks up as one to see Alan Partridge in a pinstripe suit and shiny black shoes, a bowler perched atop Brylcreemed hair, and a briefcase in his hand/my hand.

'Morning,' said Sarah, before looking down. That's Sarah all over, a prize lemon sucker. I'm sure the lads reading this know what I mean. None of her colleagues reacted either and I became concerned that the penny wasn't dropping for them. So, back straight, nose in the air, I began to march up and down.

'I'm a businessman, dontcha know!'

Nothing, so I ploughed on. 'Just doin' some business. Buy! Sell! Wanna get ma bonus.'

By now they were all looking.

'Call me Mr Corporate, y'all.' I realised that I'd slipped into an American drawl, so I tried to steer myself back to more how-do-you-do territory. 'Pull up the figures for Q4, what what.'

Shit. Now I'd become too posh, and in any case I remembered that people in business tend not to have an accent; they just speak much louder than real people.

'Did someone say "dress-up Friday"?' I bellowed, my heels clickety-clacking as I strode, or strod. (I'd deliberately moved to the tiled kitchen area to achieve this effect.)

'What?'

I stopped clattering my feet. 'Did someone say "dress-up Friday"?'

'Dress-*down* Friday.' Sarah again.

'I know that, Sarah.' There was an edge to my voice which I regret. 'I'm having some fun with you.'

'By taking the piss out of us? You think we like having to wear suits while you lot swan around in jeans?'

'I don't swan, Sarah. Don't say I swan when I don't. Yes, I wear a jean sometimes. I also wear a chino or a thick cottoned pant. But I have to be comfortable if I'm to produce the radio that, by the way, guys, keeps you all in a job.'

The atmosphere had really soured so I decided to abort. I removed the bowler hat and suit jacket. 'I've decided not to participate. Can someone return my £5, please?'

Silence. 'I'm not participating, so I'll require a refund. I shouldn't be expected to pay.'

They pretended they hadn't heard me so I approached the collection box, a locked petty-cash tin with a slot in the top. I shook it in the hope of dislodging some cash but nothing came.

'Right, one of you is opening this. You've got ten seconds.'

In unison they began to count down from ten, their voices accidentally harmonising so they sounded like one of those monk choirs from the Old Spice advert. Under different circumstances, I would have found this pleasing on the ear. But not now.

'Eight, seven, six, five . . .'

I shook the tin hard, looking for all the world like Ainsley Harriott at one of his barbecues when he's had too much punch and gets his maracas out. I stopped, determined to keep every ounce of my dignity.

'Very well. I'm happy to donate. It all goes to charity!'

'Charity?' said Sarah. 'We're putting it towards a Nespresso machine.'

I strode away. And I'll be honest, that day has coloured my opinion of charity. But while I haven't given to charity since then (this was in 2007), it isn't the reason I don't want make the Footsteps of My Father a charity walk.

The Footsteps of My Father Walk is to honour my father. Raising money or awareness for a good cause can only subtract from that. Make it a charity walk and suddenly everyone's talking about leukaemia or Terrence Higgins when they should be talking about Alan Partridge and Alan

Partridge's father. No. Charity and father-honouring are two rival, conflicting ideas, and it is essential that nothing detracts from the true purpose of this walk.

Well, no prizes for guessing how well that goes down. The general view seems to be that I am lazy or mean-spirited, but then I work with women who pass round sponsorship forms at the drop of a hat. Not *for* the drop of a hat, I might add, though I wouldn't be surprised if that's the next thing: 'My nine-year-old is going to be spending his Saturday dropping a hat to raise money for Save the Children.' Of course he is. He is one!

That said, I have nothing against charity walkers. It's a low-risk and relatively easy way to raise money, even if you're doing it in your bra or rhino costume.

Back in '85, I was sent to cover Ian Botham's walk from Land's End to John o' Groats for Saxon Radio. Alongside a phalanx of well-wishers lining the route, I was there to cheer on and grab a quick interview with the great man (Botham).

I saw him come by and, easing a couple of youngsters out of my path with a gentle forearm, I positioned myself alongside the moustachioed cricket ace.

'Alan Partridge, Radio Norwich. How are you feeling?'

'Not bad! Bit of a dicky tummy, but otherwise fine.'

'So that's what IBS stands for! Ian Botham's Stomach!' I would have said, but the line only came to me sixteen years later.

Instead, I lobbed in a prepared line: 'They call you Beefy. But you're burning 5,000 calories a day. I'll tell you some-thing, y—'

He'd turned away to sign a girl's cricket bat, milliseconds before my punchline. No matter. I waited.

After a minute or two, the girl effed off and Ian turned back. I continued: 'They call you Beefy. But you're burning 5,000 calories a day. I'll tell you something, you won't be beefy for long!'

He laughed – everyone did – then replied: 'Yeah, although it's more of a nickname. Even if I'm thin, I'll be Beefy.'

'Like jerky.'

'Pardon?'

'Beef jerky. It's thin beef. Meat, but hammered meat.'

'Ah. Like carpaccio.'

'Exactly, Ian. Or bresaola.'

'What's bresaola?'

'Like carpaccio, but thin and air-dried and red. Basically, if a cow had a scab, it would be bresaola.'

'Great talking to you,' he said as he broke into a jog, only stopping when he was about five yards ahead of me.

'Cheers, Scabby!' I called after him. 'I mean "Beefy"!'

6.

FOOTSTEPS OF MY FATHER™

***

IN THE DAYS LEADING UP to the walk, I have my assistant call Harvey's office on a daily basis. It doesn't bother me either way if this is turned into a television programme or not. I'd just like to find out if I'm going to be on camera so I know whether to pack my good comb.

Once again, and for the avoidance of doubt, the Footsteps of My Father Walk is a deeply personal journey. It's something I want to do to honour my father. And interest from broadcasters is a side issue as far as my father and I are concerned.

That being said, I've had my assistant buy up domain names.

footstepsofmyfather.com
footstepsofmyfather.co.uk
footstepsofmyfather.net
f00t5t3p50fmyf4th3r.com[43]

She, and to be fair others, want to know why the walk even needs a website. If the walk isn't intended to raise my profile, why does it need an online presence?[44] It's a good question. I just figure that if this thing does take off, I don't want some lank-haired cybersquatter to be owning the brand.

A salutary lesson: when Phillip Schofield got the *This Morning* job, giving his career a shot in the arm like a doctor might give a convulsing junkie who's got a shit career, he wanted to shout it from the e-rooftops. Bad luck, Phill. Because at the time, *phillipschofield.com* was owned by some toothless beach-dweller who scraped a living making pottery painted with images of the seaside. The site was littered with spelling mistakes and he didn't even have PayPal. Schofield – the real Schofield, the telly one with the hair like aluminium – was pretty unimpressed and demanded that the URL be given to him. Anyway, lawyers got involved and I think it only ended when Phillip paid a couple of chaps to visit

---

43 This baffled my assistant for a long, long, long time. But to men like me and James May, who can rattle off potential private reg plates using numbers instead of letters, this is perfectly clear.

44 Of course, my assistant didn't use this phrase. Instead of 'online presence' she said 'World Wide Web page'. Believe me, when it comes to the broadband age, she's very much 'dial-up with a free modem she got from a magazine'. She still asks Jeeves!

the pesky potter and beat him up a bit. That's a headache I could do without, thanks!

Then, given that I'm setting up a website anyway, I think, 'What the heck,' and for a bit of a laugh I pay a branding consultancy £12,000 to create a visual identity for the walk. With my heavy involvement and final say-so, the designers and I come up with a logo that is as compelling[45] as it is busy,[46] as snazzy[47] as it is challenging.[48]

It's hard to describe it in words but I'll try. Its central motif is a large pair of footprints with a smaller pair of footprints inside them. This represents a child's footsteps literally being *in* the footsteps of the parent. And while one of the designers insisted it 'looked like someone tracking a fucking yeti', to me it is abundantly clear what it represents. Anyway, each of the larger footprints is in a circle so they look like eyes – with a tear falling from the left one, to signify that this is an emotional journey. Look closely at the tear and it has my face inside. The circles also double as the 'o's in the word 'footsteps'. And the 'F' of Footsteps is angled forward slightly and we've drawn a rucksack on its 'back', to capture the idea of rambling. The first 's' of footsteps snakes through to the middle of the logo so it looks like a winding road. The two horizontal lines in the 'F' of 'Father' are given trails at the back so they look like go-faster stripes and give the logo a sense of movement. And then what's this at the end? Look

---

45 My description.

46 Their description.

47 Mine.

48 Theirs.

again. The 'r' at the end of Father is a partridge in flight, an abstract drawing of a bird lifted directly from the logo of the Liberal Democrats – literally the only good thing they have ever given the world – and this bird also bears my face. And then the whole thing is put in another circle and appears to be peeping over a hilltop, like a benevolent sun shining on the British countryside. It has a lot of ideas and I like that. These days too many logos have just one idea. But, as I say, this one has a lot of ideas. Loads, actually.

Sadly, this has never seen the light of day and I'm not permitted to reproduce the logo here – all thanks to a disagreement with the branding consultancy over payment. (I sought to pay a third in advance, a third on completion of the logo and a final third when I'd completed the walk and 'developed a new and lasting bond with my late father'.)[49]

---

49 In their view, the 'new and lasting bond' required to activate the final tranche of the fee was vague and unenforceable. 'Oh yeah?' I said. 'Enforce this.' And I stuck up my middle finger, momentarily forgetting we were talking on the phone. Just as well, as I'd raised my ring finger in the confusion.

7.

WALK EVE

***

'Twas the night before [Alan's walk],
When all through the house,
Not a creature was stirring,
Not even [an Alan].

THAT'S A CLEVERLY MODIFIED excerpt (and remember there's a 'p' in that word – lot of people forget that; it's 'excerpt' not 'excert') from one of my favourite poems. For me, a poem that rhymes is always superior to one that doesn't, suggesting the author has put in that little bit of extra work. And on this particular night, the words are all true. It *is* the night before my walk and I'm *not* stirring anything. Yes, I attempted to make a cheese sauce earlier, but because cheese sauce is impossible to make I've long since thrown it away. One minute it's hot milk, the next it's claggy cheese porridge. Pathetic.

My plan had been to spend the evening 'carbing up'. Pasta with cheese sauce would be followed by rice (also with cheese sauce). What remained of the cheese sauce would be mopped up with bread, each slice being used as a kind of edible baked cloth. And although in the end I didn't have any cheese sauce, I thoroughly enjoyed the meal anyway, despite it being somewhat dry (*very* dry).

Potato is another excellent source of energy-rich carbo-hydrate, so for elevenses (the p.m. ones) I have crisps in bed. The ritual of sleep-time snacking is one I'm very fond of. I'm sure you'd agree that there's nothing quite like the feeling of putting clean sheets on the bed, taking a shower and then jumping under the duvet for a lovely bag of Quavers.

The only downside, if you can call it that, is the crumbs you then have to sleep on. Personally, I'm not averse to a bit of discomfort. In centuries gone by, Puritans would birch themselves in order to be cleansed of their sins. I like to think that bedding down on a mattress lightly dusted with Quaver rubble is much the same thing. And while you might think that the Puritan approach was more unpleasant, do bear in mind that there's no stink quite like the stink of Quaver flavouring absorbed into human skin then sweated back out onto bed sheets.

Lying in bed, I decide to put in a call, or a few calls, to Harvey Kennedy's assistant, just to see what's what. Finally, I get through.

'Jemima! Just checking that Harvey's bagged a commission for the walk tomorrow? I trust there's no problem?'

'Not that I'm aware of.'

I fist-pump momentarily and hang up. And then I realise it's unclear which of the two questions she's answering. I'm not going through that again. Instead I send an email providing tomorrow's start time and location, and we shall see if Harvey comes through.

***

Well, Harvey hasn't come through, but who cares.

I awoke an hour ago after a fitful night filled with dreams of gravel that stank of cheese. A sunbeam bursts through a gap in the curtains (quite a large gap as I'd forgotten to close them). And, after a very good wash with an anti-Quaver shower gel, I'm ready – ready to walk in the Footsteps of My Father.

8.

MY ROUTE

***

I BEGIN AT MY CHILDHOOD home, 12 Cecil Road, Norwich, located now, as then, at postal code NR1 2QL. From here, my journey will take me due south, or 'south', through the last knockings of Norwich, into the resplendent Norfolk countryside and beyond.

Plunging down through Diss, Dedham Vale, Danbury and other places not beginning with 'D', I will eventually arrive at the ancient port of Tilbury on the River Thames. Crossing over to Gravesend, ideally by coracle, I will then begin the final push, passing through a series of towns that sound made up – Headcorn, Snargate, Brenzett and

Fairb[50] – eventually reaching my own personal Camelot, Dungeness 'A' power station, the place my father never managed to get to. Once there, it is to be assumed that I will crumple into a heap on the ground, my nose tenderly caressing the rich, nuclear soil, my soul finally soothed. Then I'll probably just get my assistant to drive me home.

The route, a close collaboration between myself and the AA route planner, totals 160 miles. To put that into context, if you were to refer to a thousand miles as a 'kilomile' then the trek I am about to attempt is almost one fifth of a kilomile.

To put that into context another way, the distance from Norwich to Dungeness is the equivalent of laying 25,000 London buses end to end. Not that I would ever do that, of course. With all buses removed from the capital, people would take to their cars and the traffic jams would be horrendous. Now, I'm no lover of London – if it were a person I'd want it to get deep vein thrombosis – but we each have a set of core beliefs that inform the way we live our lives. And one of mine is that you should never cripple an urban transport network. (Others include 'always give businessmen the benefit of the doubt' and 'Believe in Better'.)

---

50 This one actually is made up.

The Footsteps of My Father Walk

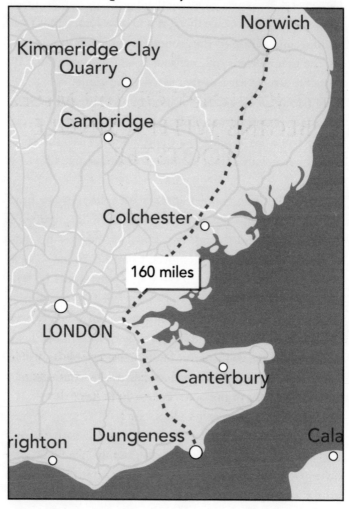

Recent estimates suggest I tend to cover roughly one metre every time I take a step (down from 1.5 metres when I was younger). That means from start to finish my walk would see me execute over a quarter of a million strides. As far as my feet were concerned, I was about to unleash hell.

9.

THE JOURNEY OF 160 MILES BEGINS WITH A SINGLE FOOTSTEP

***

DUM, DUM, DUM, DUM, dum, dum.

I am making good time and even better headway. The rhythm of footsteps drives me on, like it's the big drum of a Viking long boat or just some cox on Boat Race day.

Dum, chink, dum, chink, dum, chink.

Fernando has picked up some glass or a bit of grit and is clanking audibly. He clings to me tightly, like he used to before his mind was warped by puberty and Carol. Denise's grip is looser – she's holding on but a little less enthusiastically. But that's Denise. She can be a cold fish, unless she's drunk.

My focus now is on Fernando. He seems to be enjoying

his new noise. Slamming into the road face-first so whatever it is he's collected smashes loudly against the ground. Chink! Chink! Chink!

All the while, Denise plods onwards, truculently. Dum, dum, dum.

Dum, chink, dum, chink, dum, chink.

As a trained disc jockey, I recognise this as a potential drumbeat, specifically the one from *Saturday Night Fever*. I begin to strut, every inch a Bee Gee, making a yowling noise periodically to suggest that the new beat is painfully funky.

And now I'm picturing a young John Travolta walking his walk on a New York City sidement. I like it. Before long, I'm imagining Travolta as he is now, in a kimono and underpants, walking the same walk in a hotel suite, his eyes fixed on the terrified intern he's instructed to watch him. I snap out of it. That's the thing with imagining – you can't always choose where it leads.

I need to hurry but Denise is starting to bother me, so I kick her in the heel. It doesn't help, so I grab hold of her tongue and pull it out hard. That's better.

I should have said earlier: I've named my walking boots Fernando and Denise, after my children – Fernando and Denise. It's a corny little gesture, I know, but I take comfort in knowing they're with me, and I smiled this morning as I forced my feet into their gaping mouths. First Fernando ('Thanks, Dad'), then Denise ('Thanks for the foot, Pops').

I lift Fernando and inspect the sole for the source of the 'chink'. His rubber base is speared by a drawing pin, its shiny brass hat flush against the rubber, the spike in right to the hilt. I thank my stars I paid up for a walking boot from Hardy's of Manningtree. Had I settled for the cheap, thinner-soled Japanese boot bought from a catalogue by my assistant, the pin would have forced its way through to the main chamber of the boot, slashing and stabbing my footskin like a frenzied one-toothed shark.

I jemmy the pin out and throw it into a hedge. Then it's onwards. Like Denise, Fernando is now meeting the floor with a dum and, although less funky, the incessant dum, dum, dum, dum distracts me from my fatigue.

You wanna know something crazy? *The walk hasn't even started yet.*[51] This is merely the walk *to* the walk, because I should like the journey to commence in a very particular place.

***

To most of you, 12 Cecil Road isn't an address that will mean a great deal. And that's fine. It's not exactly seared into the public consciousness like 10 Downing Street, 11 Downing Street or the address of Sherlock Holmes. To me, however, it means more than all of those places put together. Holmes's address in particular means little to me, my mother having banned me from reading his books for much of my childhood.

Her belief was that Watson and Holmes were gay lovers. Keen experimenters and happy to take risks in the bedroom, theirs was a relationship in which nothing was off the table. And though it would seem to go against the grain of the pair's dynamic as written, Mother was certain that Watson

---

51 Nuts, huh?

was the dominant one. Not that Holmes minded. Far from it. Naked save for his deerstalker, and lashed to the bed posts with rope, he loved to be subservient and got a real kick from having all of Watson inside of him.

Regular heroin consumption, combined with a lack of knowledge about sexually transmitted diseases, only served to make the well-respected Victorian detectives hornier. Indeed, Mother was left in little doubt that the reason Holmes seemed to lack compassion as he stood over the body of the story's latest murder victim was because he was too busy salivating at the prospect of what Watson was going to do to him that night.

She also had her doubts about Mrs Hudson. Living in the flat below, can she really have been unaware of the nightly buggery marathons above? Even if we assume she didn't hear the regular role-playing sessions in which Holmes said he was a worthless piece of shit who needed to be punished – and as mother pointed out, that was a big 'if' – it seems hard to believe that the landlady wouldn't at least have noticed the thud of Holmes' body as it hit the floor, unconscious once again thanks to an over-tightened ball gag.

Yet 12 Cecil is where I grew up. It's where I learned to walk, to talk, to sing and to dance. It's also where I first dis-covered a natural flair for the hiding component of the well-known parlour game 'Hide and Be Seeked'. Many was the time I'd spend entire afternoons jammed into the smallest of spaces, barely able to suppress my laughter as my hapless parents, unable to find me, got their coats and went to the cinema or the pub to see if I'd hidden there.

More importantly, my father's journey to Dungeness had

started from here, and thus so too will mine. Or at least, that was the plan. What I hadn't realised – even though I specifically asked my assistant to check, so she must have known – is that my house is no longer there, long since yanked down to make way for a business park.[52]

With my former home now in brick heaven, I try to look for positives, and I have to say it is some consolation – indeed, in a funny way a source of pride – that rather than now being some unknown local business, my house has been replaced with the regional headquarters of Carphone Warehouse.

A less enlightened city council might have reimagined the street as a leisure centre or playground. Instead, by providing competitively priced office space to a large corporation, it has turned the land into something of real value to the community, and that gives me great comfort.

The new complex covers a large area and I am intrigued to see which bit of the organisation now calls *my* home *its* home. I'd love it to be the office of one of the senior management guys but have to accept the possibility that it may just be the men's toilets or the desk of someone in the social-media team.

But I still have a problem on my hands. What value will

---

52 I like the term 'business park', the word 'park' suggesting just the kind of freedom and fun you genuinely can have in a well-run business with a clear hierarchy. A lot of trendy tech companies have taken the word literally and installed swings in their receptions, but if your staff know where they stand and are clear as to who they can and cannot answer back to, this kind of gimmick just isn't needed.

my journey have if it isn't faithful to the key waypoints of my father's route? If my entire quest isn't to wither on the vine, I need to get into that building and start my walk from the exact grid reference of my childhood abode. No ifs, no buts, it has to happen.

'Can I help you, sir?' Here we go. It's the guard manning the entrance gate.

'I just need to pop inside.'

'Have you got an appointment?'

'I can do better than an appointment, mate – I used to live here.'

'So you haven't got an appointment?'

This conversation is going nowhere, fast.

'No, I don't have an appointment, but since when do you need an appointment to go into your own house?'

'This isn't your house. It's a business park.'

Wow. Security guards really are *terrible* at figurative speech. What I need here is someone with actual authority. Yes, I somehow need to talk to the office manager. Inserting a piece of chew gum deep into the back of my mouth, I play it casual.

'Is, er . . . is Sandra about?'

It's a calculated risk – office managers are often called Sandra.

'No one by that name here, mate.'

'Sorry, I meant Janet.'

It was a calculated risk – if office managers aren't called Sandra, they're often called Janet.

He shakes his head.

'No, not Janet, Jean. I mean Judith.'

I'm just saying random names now. Although, weirdly, it turns out there are three Judiths working there. I've never even met two Judiths, let alone known a company that employs three of them. Not that this Judith glut helps me much. Two of them aren't at work because it's a Saturday, while the other is a workflow manager and I don't think she can help me because I don't know what that is.

With access denied, I opt to begin my walk in the hut of Stu, the chap manning the entrance gate. It feels right to mark the moment with a short candlelit vigil, and I am pleased that Stu, unable to squeeze past me in order to get out, is here to share it with me. I suggest he joins me in bowing his head but he declines and that's fair enough. To our credit it's an impeccably observed five minutes' silence. At one point Stu does have to tell the driver of a car he'll be out in two tics, but I am satisfied he does so in a dignified and respectful manner.

Roughly halfway through the silence I notice the candle flame flicker. Could this be the spirit of my dead father come to wish me well on my travels? The romantic in me certainly hopes so, even if the realist knows the short blast of hot air was nothing more paranormal than Stu quietly letting off behind me. All that remains is for me to ask him to swear on his mother's life that the candle will remain lit for the entire duration of my walk, and I am on my way.

10.

AND I AM ON MY WAY

***

TOOT, TOOT! BEEP, BEEP! Honk, honk!

Well, this is nice. Like any normal man, I adore car horns, and pride myself on being able to recognise almost any vehicle currently using the British road network by its horn alone. Of course, there are those who claim that manufacturers routinely re-use the same horn noise across multiple models. I happen to disagree with this, believing that each car horn is as unique and special as a human fingerprint or a doggy's woof.

And as I set off south along Ipswich Road, the automobiles of Norwich are in particularly fine voice. The pleasing *tink, tink!* of a Ford Kuga. The playful *doo, doo!* of a Fiat Punto.

The throaty *merp, merp!* of a lorry, although I wouldn't know which kind as I don't do lorries. Yes, it's not hard to imagine how this harmless bit of fun could translate into a multi-territory early evening gameshow presented by Darren Day.

'OK, Alan, final round. Correctly identify the next horn and you'll walk away with today's star prize: a Tracker bar.'

(It may be relevant to add at this point that I was becoming peckish and had a Tracker bar in my bum's bag or bum bag.)

'Best of luck with this, Alan.'

'Thanks, Darren. By the way, I thought you were excellent as HIV-positive gospel singer Gideon in the European premiere of the award-winning USA musical *The Last Session*. But anyway, go ahead.'

Boop, boop!

'That's a Volvo S90!'

'No! It was actually a Volvo S60. Well, Alan, you don't win the Tracker bar but it's been a pleasure having you on the show and we hope to see you again one day.'

'Oh, you will, Darren. You will. I own the format, mate.'

'Everyone, give it up for Alan from Norwich!'

I take the Tracker bar out of my bum bag and begin to eat it. It's my snack and Darren Day can swivel if he thinks he can tell me when I can and cannot have it.[53] But as the Tracker merges with the saliva in my mouth and turns back into porridge, I realise there's more to these car horns than meets the eye/ear. These aren't just the everyday toots of

---

53 Thinking about it, I might replace him with Christine Bleakley. I like her. Tone down the accent a bit and she could really become something.

a male driver assisting a female driver by pointing out that she was braking too early or pulling out without looking. These toots are aimed at me. I may have planned to slip out of town quietly but it seems the drivers of Norwich have other ideas. They're giving me the car horn equivalent of a 21-gun salute. And I have to say, it warms the cockerels of my heart.

People will say I'm being too complimentary and that there's no way they're this good, but I genuinely believe that if the people of Norwich were Cheddar, they'd be Tesco Finest Cheddar. Full-flavoured and matured for four weeks, the keenly priced milk derivative has been winning the hearts (and, I believe, minds) of customers for the best part of a decade. Personally, it gives me heartburn and makes me feel like I might be sick any minute, but if you're after the market leader, look no further.

With all eyes – and horns – on me, I wonder if this is what life is like for an international movie star or Samantha Fox.[54] But soon it becomes more than just car horns. People are winding down their windows, eager to learn more about my quest. 'What you up to, Alan?' 'Where you headed, Alan?' 'Why you walking in the fucking road, Alan?'

Admittedly, that last one is less well meaning. It came from a white Ford Transit van with three men sitting in the

---

54 For the benefit of overseas readers or those under thirty, Sam Fox – full name Samantha Fox – was a topless model in the 1980s, regularly posing for the pages of the *Sun* newspaper. Widely regarded as the most beautiful woman ever, Samantha also does a lot of work for charity. Her sexual preference is lesbian.

front. As is customary, the one in the middle looks uncomfortable with the arrangement, but it's the driver who does the hollering. Not that I can quibble. With my eyes flicked to the 'closed' position (I find I'm more aurally sensitive if I pretend to be congenitally blind), I've strayed onto the road.

I avoid injury by diving to the pavement like a goalkeeper doing an ace soccer save, but I'm angry at myself. It is my belief that the roadway is for motorists. You wouldn't see a group of retired Hyundais trekking along the Pennine Way or a Lexus hot and knackered on a treadmill, so why should a walker be permitted next to a major road?

Don't get me wrong, I have no beef with walkers per se. In fact, as a driver I take great pride in not having killed a single pedestrian in over thirty years behind the wheel. But as a form of transportation? You must be kidding me, pal. Walking's for the birds (not literally). (Apart from chickens.) (And penguins.) It's a relic of times gone by, like bowler hats or gall bladders. And while I do believe in preserving the traditions of the past – and I'm talking specifically here about Morris Dancing – it must never be at the expense of road users.

No, the only reason a person should be travelling on foot next to a carriageway is if their car has broken down, they're a sex worker or they're walking in the footsteps of a close relative, such as a father.

Yet they must do so with the utmost care, and I have failed in this duty. It's clear I need to apologise. I quickly jot down the van's registration number, although only in my mind because I don't have a pen. I'm pretty sure it's 'S', something, '0', something, something, something, 'K'. I vow to verbally do right by them when I'm back on North Norfolk Digital. Whoever these men are, whether work colleagues or, and this is just as likely, gay lovers with a shared interest in Transit vans, I at least owe them this much.

***

It's important to me to say thanks to each and every well-wisher. But I don't want people to think I am fobbing them off with the same response each time. Fortunately, I'm a DJ, so words are my currency. The English language – and the French language to a far, far lesser degree – is like putty in my mouth, a single word soon becoming two, three, even four. 'Thanks' becomes 'ta' becomes 'thank you' becomes 'thank ye'. (Technically, 'thank ye' is Elizabethan but most people will still understand it, with the possible exception of tradesman and those, if any, who deny the existence of history.)

Then there's intonation. Barely used by much of the population, and deeply misunderstood by people like Loyd Grossman, skilful intonation can have a dramatic effect on how well we communicate. Just as a kindly zoologist opening the sanctuary gates gives a rehabilitated herd of monkeys their freedom, so the emphasis placed on different words gives phrases theirs. Take the phrase 'thanks very much'. There's not much you can do with that sentence, right? WRONG.

Try saying each of these aloud. It's best if you sit upright and spit out any food that may be in your mouth. If you're on a bus or a train, it's important that you still take part in this. I've taken the time to create the demonstration, so if you don't participate you're disrespecting me and you have no class.

'*Thanks* very much.'

'Thanks *very* much.'

'Thanks very *much.*'

'*Thanks very* much.'

'Thanks *very much.*'

'*Thanks* very *much.*'

'*Thanks very much.*'

How was that for you? You may be surprised at your reaction. Most likely your initial scepticism will have given way to a sense of awe, as the true possibilities of the English language unfurl before your very eyes.

Are you shaking a bit too? You might be.

Yes, you are, look. Your hand. It's trembling. Take a while to sit under a tree, maybe switching off your phone and not going to work for a few days. Things will be different now. And while most monkeys die within twenty-four hours of entering the wild, that doesn't matter because I was only using it as a metaphor. So just relax and enjoy the liberation of intonation. Or *in*tonation. Or in*to*nation. Or into*na*tion. Or intona*tion.*

Meanwhile, for those of you on crowded public transport who chose not to say the words aloud, you'll feel no different, and that's your own fault because, as I say, you lack class and are assholes.

***

By now it's mid-afternoon and I've reached the village of Swainsthorpe. Its only pub, the inexplicably named

Sugarbeet, is sorely tempting me – 'A pint of bitter and a plate of crackers, please!' – but I've already fallen behind schedule and need to push on.

The problem is my rucksack. Stuffed full of kit and protruding a clear foot above my head, it's like giving a piggyback to an unconscious teenager. In terms of pure weight, I've never carried anything even vaguely comparable. Once, after a few too many long iced teas at a BBC cocktail party, I promised to give Eamonn Holmes a fireman's lift back to his car, but my knees buckled before he'd even climbed on. I claimed it was an old squash injury, but I think I was just scared.[55]

Before I began my walk, my assistant said she'd been online and found out that not even the special forces carry packs as heavy as mine. Whether or not her internet research can be trusted is another matter entirely. This is the same woman I once caught raising her hand when she wanted to make a bid on an eBay auction.

No, I would back my own judgement on this one. I don't dispute that the pack is big. It has a capacity of one hundred litres, and though I have no intention of filling it with liquid, that still gives you some idea of its size. The South African shop assistant had urged me in the strongest possible terms not to buy it, but I'd gone ahead anyway because – and I quote – 'I'm just that kind of guy.'

Besides, in a matter of days I knew my body would grow accustomed to the weight. Bear Grylls once told me – and indeed anyone who watched that particular episode of his

---

55 Love you, Eam!

TV show – that experts believe we utilise only about 5 per cent of the body's true capability. And while I know for a fact he was confusing the word 'body' with the word 'brain', he still had a point. We *are* capable of more than we think. Consider the pensioner who manages to complete the Flora London Marathon (albeit on a mobility scooter); the successful middle-aged singleton who sets up three Tinder dates in a single week, all with women who were either quite good-looking or very good-looking; even the tiny ant who can carry weight equivalent to a human lifting – at a guess – sixty skyscrapers.

***

It's the end of day one on the Footsteps of My Father Walk and I have reached the village of Newton Flotman, some eight miles from my start point. I had hoped to get a few more miles under my belt, but I'm certain I'll soon make up any shortfall. Speaking of my belt, I notice it's incredibly sweaty under there. Some of the sweat, and I suspect it's the stuff I emitted early in the day, has solidified into a kind of black dough, flecks of which are dotted around my midriff. Yet no matter how great the temptation – and I reassure myself that it's perfectly normal to have these thoughts – there's no way I'm going to eat any of it.

My first task is to make camp. I've been looking forward to this because my new tent is an absolute stunner (or 'stonker', as Lenny Henry would say). It cost me £699.99 and is designed to withstand the kind of gusts you only find in the Arctic. The South African shop assistant said it was overkill for a trek in the UK, but I'd gone ahead anyway because 'I'm just that kind of guy.'[56]

But there's a snag. The tent is at the bottom of my state-of-the-art rucksack.

When drawing up the list of items to pack, I'd cleverly arranged things in order of where they should be placed. The first thing on the list represented the item at the top of the bag, the last thing on the list, the item at the bottom. Yet when my assistant came to do the packing . . . well, you can guess the rest.

'Hapless' doesn't even begin to cover it. Why she would think the first item on the list should be packed first, I have no idea. Who packs like that? Much like her belief in the Bible and her insistence on never allowing her petrol tank to become less than half full, it simply defies all reason.

I estimate that it will take me somewhere between twelve and fifteen minutes to unpack the bag and retrieve the tent, and there's no way that's going to happen – 'I'm just not that kind of guy.' It's then that I have a brainwave. Scrolling through my mental Rolodex I come to a stop at the name of one Tony Cloke. Tony and I go way back and had been friends until as recently as 8 June 2013. In a handy twist of fate, Tony lives right here in Newton Flotman because he can't afford to buy in Norwich. I shall borrow a tent from him.

Knock, knock, knock!

---

56 And also I thought he was saying 'attic' rather than Arctic. Like I say, he was South African.

This is me, rapping on Tony's front door. The custom when arriving at someone's house is to knock twice. And I am well aware of this. But I need help and by adding a third knock I've immediately made my presence more interesting. 'Ooh,' Tony will be thinking, 'three knocks instead of the traditional two, who could this be? I'm already feeling more inclined to help them out, unless it's the Jehovahs, in which case they can fuck off.'[57]

The door opens. Or rather, Tony opens it – it's not automatic or anything. He's more overweight than I remember but has quite a lot more hair. He looks me up and down, then up again so he's back on my face.

'Alan?'

'Hello, Tony. Long time, no text.'

'You still owe me three grand, you prick.'

Full disclosure: in early June 2013, I accidentally rear-ended Tony. (Just to be clear, I mean I rear-ended Tony's car.) (Just to be even more clear, I mean my car rear-ended Tony's car.)

Tony claimed it was my fault but I believe it was his. The lights had gone to green, so technically (perhaps even legally?) he should have pulled away. But did he? No, because he was too busy picking food out of his teeth. With his lower front incisors huddled together like cows under a tree, stuck food was a recurring problem for Tony. Whether or not this issue played a role in the collapse of his first marriage is a moot point, but if your husband is a man who can't eat a sandwich without his front teeth ending up looking

---

57 I'm afraid Tony's language can be quite fruity at times.

like they're wearing gloves made of chewed bread, then it's bound to cause friction.

Long story short, he and I had drifted apart after the incident. But he's a good man and I feel sure he'll see past all that to help out a friend in need.

'Listen, Tone, forget about the car smash, I need to borrow a tent.'

'Sure.'

I've condensed our conversation to cut out the bits that aren't relevant. But in brief, we restated our positions *vis-à-vis* the accident, he grabbed me by the throat, I smashed him in the balls, he tried to roundhouse me but couldn't, he's fifty-six, we realised this was stupid, hugged, hugged again, did high fives, hugged again, cup of tea, slice of cake, borrowed tent, hug for the road, walked away.

***

I clamber over a low fence and onto a bowling green. I've always had a soft spot for these places, and I went through a period in the eighties of having crown green bowls-related daydreams. I'd imagine myself *as* a bowling ball. I'd roll along the grass, round and round, round and round, until with a gentle 'clack' I'd bump into a smaller white ball.

'Hullo,' I'd say. 'I'm black.'

'Hello,' the white ball would reply. 'I'm white.'

Then in unison we'd say, 'And that's just fine.'

At the time, I'd been listening to 'Ebony and Ivory' a lot (a *lot*), so I guess the racial harmony thing had something to do with that. Why I'd been dreaming about crown green bowls, however, is less clear.

With a heavy heart comes the knowledge that I'm going to have to hammer my tent pegs into the hallowed turf. I'm aware this will cause significant damage but I'm too tired to look for anywhere else, and also I once read an article in the *Mail on Sunday* that said bumpy mattresses can cause sciatica.

As I remove the canvas house from its bag, I realise that it's seriously large – at least a six-berther. Tony doesn't even have kids so there's no reason for him to need a tent this size. It's all a bit 'look at me'. And while we all like to act the big man on a campsite, this is just silly. The obvious explanation would be that Tony bought the tent as part of his attempt to woo the woman who would later become his (second) wife. It was a classic piece of dick-swinging.

I begin to think about the kinds of things the two of them must have got up to in it. For a while it's immensely enjoyable, but when I imagine Tony rolling over and catch a glimpse of him front-on, I don't like it anymore and ask my mind to make it go away.

Darkness has now fallen and I set about the business of becoming erect. Strictly speaking, it takes more than a single person to put up a tent of this scale. But I'm not going to let that stop me. Not that it's easy, mind you. The tent is a stubborn old bugger. When I put the front up, the back falls down. When I put the left up, the right falls down. I'm reminded of that impossible staircase in the famous sketch by Etcher.

After four hours of trying – I nearly wrote 'crying' then! (which I did do, actually) – I quickly reach the conclusion that this isn't going to work. But as I manhandle the tent back into its bag, I stumble over something else. Hidden at the bottom is another tent. And it's a ruddy one-manner!

Under my breath I've been saying some pretty rotten things about Tony. They were just born of tiredness and hunger – *of course* I don't want him to step on a landmine – but suddenly all is forgiven. With a renewed sense of purpose, I set to work. Within minutes I am under canvas and, to quote Act IV, Scene 3 of *Henry V*, 'a-bed'.

It's only when I attempt to zip the door shut that it dawns on me that this is a tent for a child. I had seen the picture of Buzz Lightyear on the outer wall but chosen not to leap to conclusions (the *Toy Story* franchise can be enjoyed by people of all ages). But now I am inside it, the truth cannot be denied: I am in the sleeping vessel of a child. Tucking my knees to my chest, I close my eyes and get some shuteye. (Or 'open mouth', as my wife used to call it, because I sleep with my mouth agape and my tongue ululating slightly.)

11.

TODAY IS TWO DAY (I.E. DAY TWO OF MY WALK)

***

I WAKE WITH A GRUNT.

In my sleep I have unfurled, and my arms and legs are straining against the walls of the child's tent. To an outsider, I must look like an alien foetus, about to emerge from its birthing sac, albeit a sac adorned with the face of Buzz Lightyear. Buzz himself isn't looking too hot either. I can make out his image on the outside of the canvas, and with my foot ballooning one side of his smile he looks for all the world like a man with an infected abscess. 'Infinity! The final frontier!' I mutter from one side of my mouth, and chuckle at the idea of this well-loved character sporting a painful infection. Perhaps if he'd heard the 'Buzz' of an electric toothbrush once in a while, he wouldn't be in this mess!

I realise then that I've forgotten my electric toothbrush. I emit a yell that could be heard from as far afield as a far field. I *hate* forgetting my electric toothbrush. Sure, I can go to a Boots's and pick up a regular toothbrush, but non-electric toothbrushes are so lame. FML, they blow. They suck serious shit.

I furl again, releasing the strain on the tent's outer wall. This allows me to unzip the zip, unfurl once more and tumble out onto the bowling green. It's only when I stand that I realise how achey I am. My joints feel like they have gone ten rounds with Mike Tyson or simply been injected with extra gristle. My entire body is a hurt zone, a laser-questing term for when you find yourself diving for cover but then the others find you anyway and jump on you.

This is perplexing since I had set off in, or very close to, QSPC. Could it be that I've brought too much gear with me? In my left hand, I have a full-sized tent bag, complete with pegs and mallet. In my right is a map. On my back a rucksack containing clothes, foods, beddings, washbag and the survival basics – rope, first-aid kit, torch, whistle, flare and GPS. I also have pots, pans and a camping mug clanking beneath like a cork hat for my backside.

My assistant had offered to sherpa for me but, since she's close to seventy and a woman, I didn't feel comfortable taking her up on the offer.

'[My assistant],' I said to her. 'You are not a Sherpa. You couldn't sherp if your life depended on it.' Besides, you should have heard the noises she made trying to carry my microwave ovens up a staircase to my study.

No, I would carry my things. But there was no denying my body was paying the price for this bravery. Sleeping in a tent the size of a rubber johnny hadn't helped. I make a decision there and then to jettison anything I don't need on the road and have it ferried to my stopover locations by FedEx each day. I make a further decision to avoid camping.

With that decided, I bosh a few painkillers and set off in search of a good British cooked breakfast. The cooked breakfast, or 'cookie', has come to the rescue of travellers since it was invented in the War.

The gold standard as far as I'm concerned came at a hotel in Surrey where a few hundred of us had gathered to celebrate Gary Wilmot's wedding to Joanne. Gary adored a cooked breakfast and paid for brand-new fryers for the hotel on the proviso that they didn't try to do anything fancy. He wanted the classic British fry up, lots of choice and lots of oil. Everything was cooked to order – and while it did mean the bacon wasn't anywhere near crispy, that's how I like it, and believe me the limp pork slices went down a treat! No, Gary would not stand for pre-cooked items being kept warm under catering bulbs. 'I spend my life on stage under lights. I wouldn't wish that on a sausage!' And he had two different types of cooked mushrooms: a portobello and a button. I went for both! With a large portobello on one side of my plate followed obediently by a train of small mushrooms, they looked like a duck and her ducklings had been turned into fungus. Well, I told Gary this and he roared. 'You *have* to say that during the speeches.'

I obliged, but when the moment came and he broke off from saying how beautiful his wife was to tell everyone that

Alan had something to say, I remade the observation, but minus any mushrooms. As a result, people didn't really understand what I was trying to do and I lost confidence in the routine. I'd taken Sue Cook as my 'plus one', since Carol had just unilaterally ended our marriage and I felt I could use this as leverage to get close to Sue. But as my routine ended, she was just staring at me with one of those withering looks she gives.[58] I felt quite angry at Gary for putting me in that position and we didn't speak after that.

If Newton Flotman is anything like Norwich, I know I'm not going to get that level of 'cookie' here. It's a Sunday and my options are limited to greasy spoon cafes. The kind of places that don't open until 9 a.m. and harp on about their all-day breakfast – yeah, all day unless you want it for breakfast!

Luckily, Denby's is open. A small business that has been run by the same family for decades (this is a guess), it's exactly the kind of place I had hoped to stumble upon.

I love this. This is me happening on small, ordinary lives and writing about them, providing a snapshot of Britain – a bit like when Rick Stein visits cheap local restaurants run by grannies and pretends the food is as good as proper restaurants. Yes, I expect to pick up all manner of amusing vignettes.

---

58 Sue Cook and I go way back. She's a straight-talker – and how! She really will go to town on you if you displease her. I mean, she'll call you all the names under the sun. I've seen her reduce John Stapleton to tears more than once, but it's only because she cares. It's funny that she's called Sue Cook when she can't cook, but she will sue.

I sit down and peruse a menu, smiling wryly at the use of superlatives. The mega breakfast, as an example, is only the fifth-best breakfast they offer. Above that comes the double mega, the king, the best and the double best. Approaching the counter, I point out that their best breakfast isn't even their best breakfast.

'What you saying?' asks the owner. Well, I know better than to repeat what I'm saying to a man who asks me what I'm saying, so instead I try to explain to him what a vignette is. He seems annoyed, which I put down to him being busy, hot and Greek or Turkish. I order the double mega and then, still aching, I retreat to a table to lick my wounds (not literally) and apply Deep Heat (literally).

Deep Heat, for those of you not aware of the warming ointment, stinks. Its smell is very, very poor. I shouldn't have applied it in a small cafe, but it's on now so I pretend to ignore the stares and grumbles of the clientele and read a newspaper which abbreviates surnames so freely – Roo, Cor, Ger, Bur – that the headliners sound like the aroused grunts made by *Carry On* characters when they spy a buxomly betitted lady. And there was nothing wrong in that! Who doesn't make quiet noises when they become aroused by a big chest! I know I do, although with me it's more of an involuntary hum.

Breakfast arrives and I eat quickly and well, polishing off the wet items (beans, egg, tomato) while my tea cools, knowing that I'll then be able to wash down the tastier dry items (bacon, bread) using the now-drinkable breakfast drink.

And that's breakfast, bar a brief incident that's not relevant to the journey – although if you must know, I spotted a waitress there, fell in love with her, utterly in love, stayed in the cafe most of the morning so that I could just be near her, told her how I felt, she didn't wanna know, we had a chat, bit of a cry, her dad got involved and we agreed to leave it there. Might have just been tiredness but, as I say, hurt like hell at the time and knocked me for six, to be fair.

And then! Back on the road.

I hide my rucksack and tent in a hedge and send instructions to my assistant to come and collect them and then hand them to FedEx. She's not driving at the moment because her blood-pressure pills make her hands shake, but the items will need collecting today so she might have to use public transport.

She tells me that Harvey Kennedy is still uncontactable. Doesn't matter now, I tell her, but I'm a bit miffed at his manners! She tells me that his inevitable damnation to the eternal fires of hell might make him think again, and I smile at that.

And then I begin to walk. I will walk to Diss, just fifteen miles away. As chewed-up bacon and egg course through my bloodstream, I feel my aches evaporate.

***

Well, the aches are back. I've covered seven miles now, trouncing the previous day's record, but then I've not had to gain access to a business park or carry a caravan's worth of gear in a ruckbag today.

As I stroll through the village of Aslacton, I nod appreciatively at the church of St Michael, a stone and flint structure. I've always loved flint, that hard, sedimentary,

cryptocrystalline form of the mineral quartz, categorised –
certainly by this observer – as a variety of chert.

You see, Norfolk is very much the home of flint and the
home of flint homes. And flint was a substance close to my
heart ever since I'd used it as the name of a TV drama I'd
devised and had high hopes for.

12.

FLINT

***

FLINT WAS DEVISED AS a spin-off of my could-still-be-a smash-hit drama *Swallow*. *Swallow* centres on a Norwich police-cop who is very much his own man and, although it remains uncommissioned, I'm excited that it now comes with the added sweetener of a fully formed ITV2 spin-off, which for some reason TV commissioners get rock-hard for.[59]

---

59 At the time of writing, Polly Hill has taken over as Head of Drama at the much-loved commercial network and I very much look forward to a constructive dialogue with her and her team, comforted by the knowledge that the high turnover of commissioners means if she doesn't bite, her successor probably will.

I see *Swallow* occupying a primetime berth on ITV1, or ITV as it was once known and is now known again. *Flint* is pure ITV2. The colour palette will mirror that of Foxy Bingo, which is a key advertiser for the station, while – and this might just be my imagination – the volume will be higher by quite a lot. In terms of story, *Flint* will occupy the same cinematic universe as *Swallow*, but with the key differentiator that Flint is no cop. He's a fireman, or a firefighter, as firemen like to call themselves. He first appears in a minor role in episode three of *Swallow* (yet to be scripted), wiping soot from the cheek of a crying woman after Swallow has busted a jewellery-smelting racket sky-high. And that moment of brooding tenderness will leave the audience wanting more.

I won't bore you with the details – this book is about my father, not my drama portfolio – but the potted version goes thus: Flint widowed himself by drunkenly lighting a cigar in bed and then falling asleep, unaware that the burning ember would set fire to his wife's side of the bed. He awoke to find her side of the bedroom was just smouldering ash. Has his wife burned to death or has she escaped? The ferocity of the fire he slept through meant there was no way of knowing if her remains were among the charred ruins.

Unable to live with himself, Flint leaves his job as a stuntman in order to become a fireman.[60] As a late-joiner, he has

---

60 Internet message boards will light up as fans and viewers alike delight in the irony of Flint's being a fireman. Flint is used to start fires. This Flint puts them out! (Apart from the one that did for his wife.)

life skills that the rest of the brigade lack. He's also not picked up their bad habits or addiction to pornography, so he has a totally different approach to fire fighting. This makes him an outsider, but he kinda likes it that way.

Believe me, the fire has hit Flint hard. Eaten up by guilt, he is now avowedly anti-smoking, certainly of cigars. He does still drink but not in bed and not if there are naked flames around. And upsettingly, he often makes out his wife's face in the flames of a barbecue or on a slice of burnt toast and does a double-take. But when he looks again, her face has gone and it's just a brick of charcoal or some black bread. He'll also see her long auburn hair in crowds, but when he chases her and spins her round, she's just another similarly haired woman, or man, or a Red Setter dog. And that is-she-or-isn't-she[61] storyline will run in the background of the serieses. It puts a romantic kibosh on the simmering romance between Flint and his now-divorced area commander, a former school friend he hesitates to call 'an old flame' out of respect for the flames that may or may not have enveloped his wife.

He works for the Norfolk Fire Service, and although he's just a regular firefighter, he takes it upon himself to investigate arson and electrical fires and track down hoax 999 callers.

I imagine that every now and then the two shows would cross paths, revealing that they both exist within the same Swallow Universe. For example, Swallow might be discussing whether the crude oil stain they've found is actually just

---

61 Cremated.

Me with Sidekick Simon, BEFORE the walk.

The old me, pictured at work before the walk. At first glance: a man without a care in the world, goofing off with Sidekick Simon and flashing the warmest of smiles. But look closer – at the shit posture, the dead, milky eyes – and it's clear there's a void deep inside of me. (As for Simon, his inability to muster a smile is just one reason why regrettably he'll never amount to much in broadcasting.)

The yellow polo neck (sometimes wrongly referred to by its American name 'turtleneck') came in a multipack of three polo necks bought in January 2000 from a covered market. There was a baby blue one (pictured elsewhere) and a burgundy one, but I've lost the burgundy one. Interestingly, even though the polo necks came in a sealed cellophane packet, the yellow one is a different brand (Spinnaker) to the baby blue one (US Crew). Never checked the burgundy one.

Me in studio, AFTER the walk.

The new, improved me, with the poise, steel and panache that only comes from overcoming incredible adversity over a great distance. Observe the knowing gaze, the wise smile and the way the pen nestles obediently in the crook of my knuckle.

As I explain in another caption, the baby blue polo neck I'm wearing came in a multipack of three polo necks bought in January 2000 from a covered market. As I say in the other caption, there was a yellow one and a burgundy one but I've lost the burgundy one. There's an interesting story about the respective brand names of the polo necks, but I won't repeat it here because you can just read it in the other caption.

My childhood home, 12 Cecil Road, Norwich.

Long since smashed to bits by the wrecking ball, this was the house in which I spent my formative years. We had a small shed in the garden and as a young boy I used to imagine that a homeless person lived inside it. His name was Eric and he was a kindly old man who'd fallen on hard times. I felt great sympathy for him. To have ended up living rough in the autumn of one's life must be incredibly hard. At the same time, it was important not to lose sight of the fact that Eric was trespassing. And so we came to an arrangement. I would allow him to stay, but in exchange he had to do *whatever* I said (am laughing as I write this). For example, if he came to school with me and I told him to look up a teacher's skirt, he *had* to do it (really laughing now). Yes, I had a lot of fun with Eric – and I hope Eric had fun too – but by the time I reached the age of eight I'd begun playing different kinds of games and

regretfully reached the decision that Eric, poor Eric, had to be killed off. Within days of my decision, Eric informed me he had contracted throat cancer (have stopped laughing now). As an imaginary person he had no access to the NHS and so had no choice but to retreat to the shed and take matters into his own hands. On 3 October 1966, Eric placed a shotgun in his mouth and pulled the trigger. A tragic end to a tragic life. He is survived by his wife Elsie (also imaginary).

Municipal swimming pool, Norwich. (*Opposite page*)

This photo was taken during the filming of my 2012 documentary *Welcome to the Places of My Life*. I include it not only because it features the swimming pool in which I did much of my pre-walk training, but also because it makes me look quite buff. I'm a relatively tall guy with decent muscle tone and when the light catches me at the right angle I've every reason to be proud of the way I look.

For those of you reading this book with young children, I should point out that I am not naked in this photograph. As is traditional in the UK's swimming baths, my bum, balls and pecker are hidden underneath a pair of waterproof underpants or 'trunks'. You will find full-frontal nudity in the changing rooms, but I make no apologies for that – a man has to get clean. And when a man's clean, a man then has to get dry. Leave the leisure centre with a damp crotch and, believe me, you're opening the door to all sorts of medical problems – a moist, warm groin being the perfect incubator for germs and mould spores alike.

Footsteps of My Father logo.

The design agency that helped me with the brand identity refuse to grant me permission to reproduce the original here, so this is very much my stab at it. Bear in mind, this is sketched from memory and also I'm not a very good drawer because I have a bad hand after I slammed it in a microwave door. But all the key ingredients are there – the footprints that double as weeping eyes, the snaking road for an S, the final R redolent of a bird taking flight. You'll also notice a tiny rugby ball sailing over the capital H, because I realised it looked like rugby posts. Although I forgot to mention it in the text on pages 77-78, the rugger ball was an idea I did ask to be included. Coming up with new typographical ideas had got me so excited I'd started devising ones that didn't actually pertain to my walk, and this was the point at which my relationship with the designers finally fractured.

Me, in front of the Carphone Warehouse offices in Norwich and the site of my childhood home.*

It's a lovely feeling when you find out the place where you spent your first Christmas is now regional HQ for a mobile phone company, especially one like Carphone Warehouse with its market-leading quad-play offering. I've even done a few motivational talks for them over the years.

They normally invite me to stay on for the cocktail reception afterwards, and I'm happy to do so. I've loved cocktails ever since discovering *Sex & The City* a few months ago, and with my speech over I'll consume four or five in pretty short order. It's at this point I'll order my taxi, giving me a further ten minutes to have two or three more before heading home. It means I enjoy every drink on the menu, yet by the time I begin to be unwell I'm off Carphone Warehouse property and in the back of a taxi. The cabbies don't like it, and I can appreciate why, but at the end of the day there's absolutely nothing they can do.

* And the first of several photos into which I've paid a GCSE design student to Photoshop me. I was sadly unable to publish the selfies I'd taken on the journey because my face was too red. Seems when I walk I go very, very red indeed. Incredibly red. I looked so red!

Newton Flotman, the village where I spent a night camping out in a Buzz Lightyear tent.

A pleasant enough village – although it doesn't have a shop, which is a bit odd. One of the locals told me that Newton Flotman's claim to fame is that 16th century humanist writer and mathematician Thomas Blundeville once lived there. He offered to tell me more but I asked him not to. I've never heard of Thomas Blundeville and didn't want to clog my brain up with facts about him in case it meant I then forgot some other, better facts.

The church of St Michael in Alsacton.

A lovely building, this, and one of only 185 round-tower churches in the whole of England. There's also an old windmill there and that's round too. So quite a lot of round things in Alsacton. And I'm pointing that out because it's interesting, not because I'm scrabbling for things to say about the place. That said, fans of Ordinance Survey grid references will find Alsacton at TM156911.

There aren't a heck of a lot of amenities in Alsacton, but the village does have a primary school. And because there are less than 450 people living there, capacity is never a problem. Yes, a far cry from the crowded conditions of London's primary schools. If you're struggling to get the hang of reading and writing – and I'm afraid it does happen from time to time in Norfolk – it's no problem, you can just stay behind for a year or two. One local told me there are some pupils who are in their 20s, although he may have been pulling my leg because he was a bit of an asshole.

Kids' TV presenter Steve Backshall.

There aren't many people who can pull off a vest like this. And Steve Backshall is certainly not one of them. Yes, his biceps look pleasant enough, and it's no surprise that he often texts photos of them to female admirers and relatives. But the towel is a real mis-step. Whether it was his idea or that of his photographer, I've not been able to find out (have left messages with his agent), but basically it looks like he's flossing the back of his neck. Quite unexpectedly I bumped into Backshall twice on my journey, the second time for a live

appearance on *The One Show*. He spends so much of his life in hot, humid rainforests that you'd assume he stinks. Far from it. I found his aroma to be really quite enjoyable. If I had to compare it to anything I'd have to go with uncooked pastry.

One of the most noticeable things about Steve is that he's incredibly, almost eerily, smiley. If we assume that he's a Christian – and I do – then it may well be that he smiles when a particularly droll piece of scripture pops into his head. I have a Christian on my staff and it's something she does regularly (annoying).

Edmonds.

So familiar is his face that people rarely stop to look at the guy, meaning his preposterous appearance is given a free pass. Well, not today. Because I invite you to inspect him with me now. The flaxen locks that defy both gravity and fashion

sense are dyed that colour, a secret style choice he might – *might* – get away with were if not for his dark beard.

I once found a notebook belonging to Edmonds in which he'd sketched potential new hairstyles, each bigger and fluffier than the last. Next to them, he'd calculated the amount of hairspray required to scaffold the hair and keep it from dropping. Well I thought this was priceless but he insisted there was nothing stupid about the lift-to-weight equation he used and claimed it was first created in the 16th century by art whizz Leonardo Da Vinci. I simply don't believe him.

black phlegm caused by smoke-inhalation. 'Well,' Swallow might say. 'Let's see what the fire service think.'

There'd be a fireman in the room with his back to camera. The camera would zoom in on this mystery fireman's back, and he'd start speaking. 'Did someone say . . .'

Then he'd turn and finish the sentence: '. . . fire service?'

At that moment we'd see it was Flint. The audience, not expecting to see him on ITV's flagship channel, would exclaim, 'Shit, look. It's Flint!'

Other episodes would see Swallow finish a conversation in the pub, down his IPA and leave . . . at which point we'd make out a figure in the background. 'Shit, look. It's Flint, drinking bourbon and looking at the fireplace, with wet eyes.' There's no mention of it in the script, though. It's just one for the eagle-eyed fans, a fascinating overlap of different strands of the Swallow Universe. Also, because Flint didn't speak in this scene, we'd be able to secure the actor that day for a discounted rate.

Although they share many of the same Conservative values, Swallow and Flint are too pig-headed to see this. And their superficially different traits mean they're doomed to dislike each other, even though they might share a grudging respect now and then.

Different traits? Yes, because whereas Swallow is very cerebral and likes higher-brow hobbies such as puzzle books and word searches, Flint is all about his physicality. He spends hours in the woodland behind his home hacking at long grass with a bread knife, and on the anniversary of his wife's death/disappearance he'll go to a (safe) fight club above a pub in Yarmouth (where they wear head guards and cushioned mittens) and deliver an almighty beatdown to a confused colleague: 'Christ, Flint. I thought we were friends!' Flint has a self-destructive streak, always hurting those he gets too close to.

A note here: Flint keeps himself in shape. You'd never catch him at a gym or racquets club, but it's clear he leads a pretty physical life when you see him with his top off, which only adds to his mystery. He's in his fifties but has hardly any droop to his body whatsoever. Nor is his skin slack. There's a solid tightness to his torso. He has broad shoulders, but his arms are lithe and supple rather than bulky. Keen observers will glimpse the odd ripple in his forearms but they're arms that *suggest* muscle rather than *boast* it. His pectorals on the other hand are something to behold and, if you'll forgive me, will dampen knickers across the country. They exude strength and power. And while he doesn't shave his chest, he is only lightly haired rather than beset by matted, thick coils of body hair. No way does Flint use sunbeds or tanning lotions, yet he has a warm tone to his skin. It almost shimmers. He also has long, flint-coloured hair (I should have said that earlier), which he only lets down when he plays his drums at home. Yes, Flint is fantastic to look at.

Still, it's no skin off my nose if ITV do or don't commission the shows. I get to watch them anyway by imagining the stories and playing them out in my mind. It's ITV's viewers and potentially big-spending advertisers who'll miss out. They can make do with *Doc Martin* for all I care! And while the twin-commission would see me garner a hefty production fee, along with a pretty tasty back-end, I'm already financially solvent and have made all my monthly mortgage repayments bang on time, apart from one. So you see, I'm pretty sanguine about the show's future, with or without a commission. Couldn't give a fat frig, mate!

13.

DIGS IN DISS

***

I'VE ARRIVED AT DISS. My feet and legs hurt but the mental battle is won. Road 0, Partridge 1. And Partridge goes through to the next round! Partridge! Partridge! Partridge! Par-tridge, he's our man! If he can't do it, no one can! Iiiiii-iiiiiiiiiiiiiiiiit's PARTRIDGE! I realise I'm chanting out loud so I pack it in, quick-style. You're not in the shower now, Alan! But yes, I'm extremely happy.

I locate my digs for the night. It's a B&B on Denmark Hill. I knock at the door with a rat-a-tat-tat (actually just a rat-a-tat, thinking about it). A voice is heard through the door.

'Yes?'

Straight away, this annoys me. The British bed and break-fast used to be the envy of the hospitality world. The weary traveller would be met by a buxom middle-aged woman with ruby red cheeks and good cheer, and the only thing saucier than her humour would be the actual sauce she served with her award-winning cooked breakfasts. A B&B owner was, by definition, a customer-facing role. But try telling that to the nervous nellies who run today's guesthouses and only speak from behind locked doors or lob in chippy responses to perfectly constructive TripAdvisor criticism.[62]

'Yes?' she repeated, as I paused to think the above paragraph.

'Partridge.'

'Who is it?'

'Partridge.'

'What was it you wanted?'

Bear in mind, the door is still closed. I'm face to face with the door-knocker as a voice murmurs out from behind it, making it seem like I'm conversing with a talking brass lion.

'I've hurdurgurdur the Bradford & Bingley hmmg-mmmffnnrr,' I mutter quietly.

'Pardon?'

I repeat the above. (Can't be bothered to retype it.)

She tuts loudly and the door opens. I knew this would work. Quiet gibberish always gets them.

'I said, "What was it you wanted?"'

I shake her by the hand. 'I've come to check in and I'm

---

62 With the emphasis on constructive. If your lounge stinks of cat, you need to Febreze it. The lounge, not the cat. Although either would work.

delighted you've finally bothered to open the door,' I say, striding past her and into a lounge where three men are watching football.

'Next door,' she says.

I quickly leave. Although this was a private residence, I stand by everything I wrote above.

Next door, I'm greeted by the owner of the guesthouse. I introduce myself – 'Alan Partridge' – and she tells me her name is 'Mrs' Lancashire in that guarded way people of a certain generation tend to – as if my introduction is an elaborate form of phishing, and by telling me her first name she's divulging online banking login details. Absolutely ridiculous.

Although neither buxom nor saucy, Mrs Lancashire is at least socially functioning, unlike her neighbour. She shows me to a room that is small, clean and bright – much like herself, although I can't vouch for her cleanness – and I make myself at home.[63]

Entering my room, I see that FedEx has delivered my rucksack. 'Oh good,' I say, and she grumbles that she doesn't normally accept deliveries for guests, pulling such a face about it you'd think I'd delivered excrement through her letterbox rather than a rucksack to myself.

But she soon cheers up. Once I've settled in, she offers me tea and eventually agrees to draw me a foot-bath using the washing-up bowl that some people have in their kitchen

---

63 Almost too at home! After toileting, I accidentally walk into her bedroom. She isn't in it, I hasten to add, so I have a quick snoop and find no male shoes, which suggests there's no Mr Lancashire on the scene unless he's a cross-dresser or double amputee of the legs.

sinks as a kind of plastic inner-sink.[64] My feet, although not blistered, are practically bleating for succour.

As my feet relax (and bleed a little) into the warm water, I strike up some chat, keen to learn more about this hopefully fascinating local character. Ten minutes later, I realise Mrs Lancashire is not fascinating. She used to work for the council and now she doesn't (cool story, bro). I ask if she knows who I am, and go on to explain the overarching concept of my radio show, run through some of my TV work and perform some of the radio adverts she might have heard me in. 'If your van's off the road, the only thing you're driving is your business . . . into a wall! So call Vantastic and save yourself some propa bovva.'

Nothing. And that's fine. This is Diss, after all, an area untouched by the worlds of entertainment and celebrity, where the people have little chance of knowing who is famous and who isn't. I know that Rick Wakeman lives in Diss and he frequently complains that when he stands on a pub chair and booms, 'I'm Rick Wakeman and my glass is dry,' no one ever buys him a drink. Even though he's the keyboard player from Yes and they're just ordinary people who live in Diss.

So I don't take her ignorance personally. Until I reach the foot of the stairs and see a chilling display. On the wall, under a laminated banner that says Hettie's Wall of Fame (oh, so it's Hettie now, is it?) is a whole bevy of signed photos from previous guests, snapped next to Hettie/Mrs Lancashire.

Charlie Dimmock giving a thumbs up, Kelvin MacKenzie (who's written 'Lovely B&B and that's The Truth!'),

---

64 Never known why.

Everest Windows' Craig Doyle and lovely wife Doon, Gloria Hunniford with a glass of wine, Duncan Goodhew ('Keep swimming!'), Glenys (and Neil) Kinnock, Clare Grogan, Paul Gambaccini ('Thanks for everything and sorry'),[65] a Krankie, Jarvis Cocker . . . and in the middle of them all, a soft-focus publicity shot, all twinkly eyes and bouffant hair, stirring a feeling in me that was simultaneously like a punch in the gut and a kick in the cock. There, smiling at me, was Edmonds.

---

65 Of course, I'll never know what the DJ and music historian had done wrong. Perhaps he'd soiled his sheets? Snored loudly? Made a pass at her? Maybe he got FedEx to deliver a small bag to him. Gambo, if you're reading, get in touch! Let us know!

14.

EDMONDS

***

PEOPLE HAVE ALWAYS ASKED ME, Why do you hate Edmonds?[66]

It makes me laugh. Ha![67] I don't hate Edmonds. I don't give a shit about Edmonds. I hate the things he does, sure. I hate the way he behaves. I hate his personality and his appearance. But hate Edmonds himself? No, sir. Wouldn't give him the satisfaction.

Our paths first crossed back in the late eighties at a Christmas cocktail party hosted by Our Price radio. I was one of

---

66 I won't dignify him with his full name. Besides, he signs his emails and legal letters 'Edmonds', so he started it.

67 See?

the leading presenters on the popular instore-only station and, as such, was one of the first to arrive. Edmonds was already there and I strod over to say hi.

'Alan Partridge!' I announced, shaking his hand quickly and well.

Edmonds made some comment about us being unfashionably early. Ting! My brain snapped into comedy mode. 'I guess that makes you the First Noel!' I quipped.

He didn't crack a smile. 'What?'

'The First Noel. Because it's the name of a Christmas song and also because you're one of the *first* here and your name's *Noel.*'

'You're saying No-el. My name's Noel.'

'I know that, Noel. But the song is the First No-el.'

'What song?'

'The First Noel.'

'There's no such song. I'd have heard of it.'

'There is such song, Noel.'

'Sing it, then.'

'Fine. I just need to remember how it goes.'

'You don't even know it.'

'I do know it, I just find it hard to remember melodies when I'm flustered.'

I launched into the song but still hadn't remembered the note sequence and ended up repeating the opening line again and again, in the hope of landing on the correct melody. By the twentieth attempt a crowd had formed.

'What's he doing?' said one woman.

'Absolutely no idea,' said Edmonds, laughing, and he walked off.

In many ways, this was his first Gotcha. A successful TV and radio star humiliating an impressionable young DJ for sport. It takes a special kind of pillock to do that.

And that was merely the beginning. In 1991, the *Radio Times* had a big bash to celebrate the deregulation of TV listings, which meant that, for the first time, the popular telly mag could publish listings not just for BBC channels, but for all major terrestrial, cable and satellite television channels in the UK. It was a seismic and hugely emotional event – several of the staff were in tears – and I believe it called for a little decorum. Not Edmonds. I was there with Carol and he kept bringing her glasses of wine even though I'd said repeatedly, 'I think she's had quite enough, Noel!' He'd nod as if to say, 'Right you are, Alan,' and then I'd turn round and he'd be bringing Carol a fresh glass of the wine I'd specifically said was off limits.

That night, after Noel had royally torpedoed my chances of presenting *Win, Lose or Draw* by sniggering every time I offered my services to the show's producer, I got Carol home and – would you believe it – she was sick on the horseshoe-shaped mat that circles the foot of the toilet. This mat was quite new so needed scrubbing before a spell in the washing machine. And who do you think did the scrubbing? Was it Edmonds? No. It was Alan Partridge.

Incidents began to rack up. I agreed to commentate on a sheepdog display at the Norfolk Country Show. Edmonds had been booked to MC the closing concert that night, headlined by T'Pau, who were pretty much my favourite rock band at the time.

Halfway through the display, just as a dog was about to

force some ducks up a ramp to the raised Wendy house they lived in, an almighty *whoomp* filled the sky. It was Edmonds in what he called his Noelicopter (actually just a helicopter). He was flying low, far too low, and I knew the ducks were about to spook.

Sure enough, two of them jumped down from the ramp – while I screamed, 'Edmonds, climb! Edmonds, climb!' into the microphone, which caused people near the speaker some distress – and it took another minute for the sheepdog to get them back up, by which time Edmonds and his chopper had landed. I looked on as Carol Decker, the lead singer of T'Pau, hopped out, and they ran into the hospitality tent together before the rotors had even stopped whirring. They were both laughing their heads off.

Another time, he skidded in a gravelly car park, which fired fragments of shale in the direction of my car. None of it hit, thank God, but I was and am furious with him.

On another occasion, he found where I was holding my fiftieth birthday bash and, to sully the ambience, booked an all-male strip troupe,[68] who frolicked around me dressed as American cops – even though the theme was 'Louis XIV' and Noel knew that.

But the nadir in our relationship came in a small room at the BBC. This was 1994 and, as presenters of live shows (him, the critically mauled *Noel's House Party*; me, the critically reviewed *Knowing Me, Knowing You with Alan Partridge*), we were obliged to attend a safety tutorial for an afternoon.

Well, Edmonds made it clear he didn't want to be there and spent the first hour chewing gum and snorting whenever I put my hand up to ask a question or make a suggestion or agree with something. Nick Ross was there as well, and while I usually have a lot of time for Nick, he was trying to show off in front of Edmonds and acting like a complete arsehole, sniggering and saying, 'Yeah, Noel,' whenever Edmonds made a snide comment.

After an hour, the tutors closed the curtains and we were instructed to watch a safety video. Edmonds thought this was soooooo beneath him. He thinks he knows all about safety even though he's reckless enough to pilot helicopters while listening to the *Airwolf* theme tune on a Walkman.

As soon as the lights dimmed, Edmonds stood up to go to the toilet (and no doubt fluff up his bouffant), which I thought was disrespectful to the course leaders, Gary and Larry.

'Sit down and watch the damn video, Edmonds,' I hissed.

---

68 Doubly insulting was the fact that he'd tracked down and hired Hot Pants, the very dance troupe I had erroneously invited onto my television chat show years earlier having not realised that they were male exotic dancers and therefore totally inappropriate for a (predominantly) straight audience. The oversight had caused a stink among BBC top brass and not a little embarrassment to yours truly, which Edmonds knew full well. And there they were suggestively waggling truncheons (both types) in my face as I sat in my hired finery. Side note: now older, wiser and saggier, Hot Pants still perform today but currently trade under the name Rs, purportedly because their members – Ruud, Reggie, Rowan, Rory and Raffy – all share that initial, but more likely because Rs sounds like 'arse' and, as gay men, they find this amusing, a theory supported by their promotional material, which features a photograph of them in leather chaps, all pointing at their own buttocks and pouting. I bet Edmonds finds them hilarious.

He pursed his lips into a homosexual 'ooh' shape and sat down as the video flickered into life. Music started and then something started to dawn on me.

'Actually, Noel,' I said. 'You can go to the toilet. I've changed my mind. If you want to go, go. It's fine, actually.'

'Like he needs your permission,' snorted Nick Ross. Oh *fuck off*, Nick.

The opening music was ending.

'Really, Noel. Honestly.'

But Edmonds just sat there, looking at me, with his stupid Ewok head. The music was over and then I heard a familiar voice from the video: 'Just think! T–H–I–N–K. Think! T! Think about the dangers. H! How should I approach them? I! I'm the one responsible. N! No excuses. K! Know whatcha doing!'

I closed my eyes as Edmonds's widened. The man's voice was mine. It was me. In a cruel twist of fate, the tutors had unwittingly put on a video fronted by me, one of a number of instructional and corporate videos I'd put my face to over a Bank Holiday weekend the previous year. A friend, Arlo Gee, owned a corporate video company, Arlo Says Action, and offered me the gig, saying the fee was high and the time commitment low. So in a TV studio he'd built in a converted barn, we managed to knock out ten videos in three days, including: *Be the Best Fire Warden*, *How Leaders Lead (and How Losers Lose)*, *Identifying the Cancer that Is Low Workforce Morale*, and *Tell Me about Debenhams*.

But *Think!* was the one I'd really thrown myself into, and the folly of that was now becoming apparent. For Edmonds, this was like Christmas had come early. I felt my rectum shrink back into me with embarrassment, not least because for a cash bonus I'd rewritten some of the scripts to lend them some pizzazz and make them more memorable.[69]

Edmonds put his feet up on the table and folded his arms, and for the next hour he roared with laughter at my nascent TV work. At one point he saw former Radio 1 DJ Mike Read walk past the door, and Edmonds invited him in even though Read didn't even work at the BBC anymore and had moved on to Gold, or Classic or something – one those other commercial stations with names that sound like a chocolate bar.

Read, Edmonds and (very much the Hammond of the three) Ross sat there and laughed at me every time I looked stern in a close-up or attempted an expansive gesture or shouted, 'Think!'

I just watched them. It was an open secret that Read was a bit of a wally (this was before he outed himself as one by writing reggae songs for far-right political parties) and, of course, Edmonds was Edmonds. I felt fury building in me and eventually bolted from the room just as the closing recap song started. (All the videos ended on a song, another

---

69 This was something I did quite a bit of early in my career. I remember amending marketing material when I was at Saxon Radio in Bury St Edmunds and realising I had something special. The blurb about my show was littered with over-familiar references to 'Alan', and I was changing them all to 'Partridge' or 'Mr Partridge' when I became aware that I was also slightly improving the copy itself. For example, I changed the phrase 'latest chart music' to 'freshest pop sounds' and 'the best of our output' to the 'cream of our discharge'.

idea of mine, which in hindsight was a stupid and actually quite childish thing to do.)

To this day, Edmonds takes great delight in bringing up my corporate video work, seemingly certain he's never produced anything as embarrassing in his career. Er, *Noel's HQ*?

In summary, Edmonds is a total wazzock of a guy and I cannot stand him. But do I hate him? No.

***

And here I am, in the hallway of a woman who claims to be utterly oblivious to my career yet has a photographic shrine to my broadcasting nemesis. Still, this journey isn't about me and my career achievements and whether or not I or they are properly recognised. It's always been – and I don't know how many more times I have to say this – about *my father*.

The next morning I quickly TripAdvise, warning travellers against staying at this B&B and suggesting the owner gen up on local radio stars – and then post it online via her own Wi-Fi. Using a hotel's own wireless internet to slam it on TripAdvisor is such a sweet thrill it damn near gives me a boner, and today is no exception, although with the bulk of my body's blood busying itself in the lower legs to help them recuperate, there isn't enough in the loins to bone me up as well!

The breakfast, however, is excellent. And as soon as the FedEx driver has arrived to collect my things, I wave bye-bye to 'Hettie' and take my leave.

15.

QUITE SIMPLY, COWS

***

DAY THREE. TODAY I plan to walk eighteen miles, to Codden-ham, where I expect an apt and well-deserved dinner of 'cod and ham', if such a delicacy exists. Just as I marked the start of my journey with a candled vigil, so I like to mark the start of each day with a short announcement. It's a kind of mantra I say out loud that centres me mentally and emo-tionally and acts as a starting gun for the day ahead. And yes, some people might find that self-indulgent or pompous, but is it any more indulgent/pompous than, say, Justin Webb saying, 'I *am* the World Wide Webb' into a men's room mirror before presenting the *Today* programme each morn?

No, it isn't. My mantra is simple. Nothing formal, nothing

fussy, I simply look up to the sky and say: 'Pray silence, for I will now walk . . .'

Then a pause.

'In the footsteps . . .'

Then another pause.

'Of my father.'

Except the intonation of the word 'father' is elongated and goes low to high. Quite straightforward, really, you can do it with me now: tuck the chin in to the chest, imagining you're Brian Blessed if that helps, and give me a nice, deep, 'Faaa.' Then, lifting the head up and back, a slightly higher, 'Therrr.'

Once again. Head down: 'Faaa.' Head back: 'Therrr.'

Last time. Nice and low: 'Faaa.' Up a register: 'Therrr.'

And the full sentence: 'Pray silence, for I will now walk in the footsteps of my

faaa

therrr.'

Good. And silence.

It's a ritual that never fails to move me. And while both I and my publisher are wary of my overstating things, I can't ignore the fact that there is a genuine majesty to the way I perform it. If you don't believe me, ask the animals. On this particular morning my audience is a field of cows. These simple creatures, whose milk we cherish and whose beef delights us, are going about their normal, everyday business when I begin to speak. But as the words leave my mouth they all stop what they're doing and, to a cow, look over at me.

Without wishing to put words into their cud-filled mouths,

it's as if they're saying, 'You're a good man, Alan. With a good heart, and a good soul. You're also smarter than average and can often guess the end of thrillers before they happen. So keep doing what you're doing, keep walking in the footsteps of your father, and if the naysayers try to belittle or undermine you, they can go fuck themselves.'

Wow. These cows really don't mince their words (unlike their bodies). And while I do have reservations about the way they express themselves, I'm grateful for their support.

Just south of Diss, I cross the county border, leaving behind Norfolk, the place to which I owe everything. I look back and wave. A car driver thinks I'm hitchhiking and stops a few yards down the road, so I quickly hide in a hedgerow until he's gone then plunge into Suffolk.

16.

A FEW WORDS, THEN, ON NORFOLK

***

NORFOLK HAS IT ALL, its pastoral life a world away from the colourlessness of its county neighbour.

When sneery city people apply the word 'culture' to Norfolk, they usually prefix it with 'agri', 'horti' or 'it doesn't have any'. But if they bothered to open their eyes for a second, they'd see how thick they'd just been.

We're not just a proud hardworking people famed for our rich history and political might. We're a liberal bunch with an artistic bent, or better still, 'artistic leaning'.

Yep, Norfolk is a cultural hotbed – a heaving, teeming, writhing morass of bodies and brains that is literally groaning with culture, but without the upsetting mental image that that creates. (The only writhing bodies you'll find in Norwich are in the backstreet men's clubs that continue to blight parts of the city centre, thanks in full to a Labour-run council.)

As one of the first *county* councils to allow library users to access the internet for free, Norfolk is in a constant state of download, letting in ideas and influences from all over the world, so long as they respect our way of life and don't expect a free ride at our expense.

So what's on the menu, Alan? Well, loosen your belt a couple of notches, put on a head restraint and allow me to slip a funnel into your mouth and force-feed you a cultural feast that'll leave you happy and fat.

Take dance. The county's ethnic profile and strict highway code means you'd be hard pushed to find any 'street dance' here, but Norfolk folk sure like to move. Outsiders would have you believe the only dancers you'll find here are Morris dancers, and while, yes, there are hundreds and hundreds of them, Norfolk's flat terrain means you can spot them from a distance and steer clear if you find them annoying or infantile.[70] No, our dance roster is pretty varied: tap, modern, jazz and disco are still performed creditably and enthusiastically. And I had a brilliant time at a *céilidh* (Irish hoedown) recently before we were ejected, as they were selling booze without a licence.

If theatre turns you on, swing by one of Norwich's theatres for big-budget touring productions of a play or (for women) a musical. Or venture to an am-dram production in

---

70 I happen to love them and will often join in.

a town civic centre if you prefer your performances louder and slower. Every so often, our schools will cancel a weekly step aerobics class and use their hall to host a visiting theatre production about issues or tribesmen.

If you get your kicks from tapping your feet to the tuba or timpani, then set sail for Norfolk at your earliest convenience, because we're ace at orchestras. The 'Norwich Phil' is what we call the Norwich Philharmonic Orchestra. We do that because by saying 'Phil' instead of 'Philharmonic Orchestra' we save ourselves time. Although by explaining that I've now lost time. And I'll be honest, that's irritated me.

The current season is as jam-packed as ever at the Norwich Phil, with recitals of pieces by composers that readers are unlikely to have heard of. And if that sounds patronising, it isn't. The Phil seems to delight in choosing works by complete unknowns. To my mind, no classical composer can really be considered a success until one of his pieces has been used on an aftershave advert. That aside, a night out at the Phil still comes highly recommended. And why not team it up with an early evening dinner at one of Norwich's excellent nosh houses, or 'restaurants' as they're often known?

'Foodies' will be pleased to learn that Norwich offers few of the chain outlets that have come to blight town centres in the rest of the country. Why? Because the people of Norfolk like to do things their own way. We steadfastly say 'no' to the homogenisation of our high streets. Indeed, we have a very successful campaign group that fights tooth and nail (and plenty of other body parts besides) to keep Norwich more or less free of faceless multinational brands. For those interested in getting involved, meetings take place every Friday morning in the Starbucks on St Stephens Street.

Art fans, if any, should take a trip to Holkham Hall, where the Earl's collection of paintings attracts visitors from far and wide and high. Don't forget to check out the gift shop, where you can probably find some of these works rendered in the form of a tea towel. It's a sad fact that many visitors choose to take home and stain these masterpieces with bacon grease and soap suds, but if it boosts awareness of British art, I'm all for it.

Thanks in large part to the work of the National Trust, the UK's most important charity, our county is also blessed with a long list of magnificent period buildings. One thinks of the Blickling Estate, Oxburgh Hall and, of course, the Horsey Windpump, one of East Anglia's best-loved drainage windmills. What better way to spend a summer's day than to visit one of these historic sites before parking up in a layby to take your warm picnic out of the boot? Perfect.

That all said, it's pop and rock music that's really put Norfolk on the cultural map. Big-hitting Queen drummer Roger Taylor is from Norfolk, as is Britney prototype Cathy Dennis. Hear'Say rocker Myleene Klass is from the county, so too is Gorleston-born Hannah Spearritt, former S Club 7 singer and someone I'm proud to call a friend.

I remember in 1982 seeing a performance by the Ants. It was supposed to be Adam and the Ants, but Adam was stuck in traffic. And as they belted out an instrumental version of 'Stand and Deliver', I remember looking around the packed arena and just shouting, 'CULTURE!!!!'

For a real treat, forget everything you think you know

about folk music and get your backsides down to the Boxley Wheatsheaf on the second and fourth Sundays of every month. By day, they're just six guys named Graeme, Phil, Graham, Martin, Andrew and Rick, plus sometimes a woman called Caroline. By night, they are Will o' the Wisp, for my money the cultural highlight of the county. For the ill-informed, WOTW are a witty folk group whose perky musicianship will make you forget about the food (not very good) and who make up lyrics that gently mock the regulars. These guys are funny – real groinwreckers – but get there before Phil gets too drunk as his tipsier lyrics can sometimes cross a line, especially towards women.

These cultural nuggets might seem small and insignificant, like so many tiny stones. But pile them up, load them into a high-pressure nozzle and they will pebble-dash the face of the county of Norfolk. We're also good at poetry.

***

Day four and I'm strolling through Claydon, still able to taste last night's dinner of cod and ham[71] as I wend my way down the Norwich Road. It's a narrow road for a town of this size and the speed of the traffic is slow, and I enjoy imagining that I'm walking at the self-same velocity at which my father might have driven.

Then I see it. I stop dead in my tracks, quickly open my ruckie, search for something and then find it (takes about forty-five minutes) – it's one of the receipts I'd found in my father's items. I hold it up so that in my eyeline the words on

---

71 Battered fish and a battered sausage from a chippy.

the top of the receipt sit alongside those on the sign above a convenience store. I scan left and right, cross-referencing that their names match *exactly*. They do: Brown's.

It's where my father stopped for refreshment all those mornings ago. And here am I now, those refreshments echoing down through time like noisy, time-travelling food.

Seconds later and I'm in the shop. It appears to be a family-run operation, with a good range of produce, plus some pleasing relics of times gone by: a convex mirror high up above an aisle where today a security camera would be, a chip-and-pin card machine rather than the contactless variety (which someone once told me can switch off pacemakers), and a window that's used to let in light rather than merely house posters for providers of cheap foreign calls.

I walk in and mooch around, soaking up the history of it all, a wistful smile playing on my dry lips (I'll buy a can of Lilt as well). I find a refrigerator display, containing milk, cheese and sandwiches. I'm certain Pops would have bought sandwiches, so I stand there and just look at them, and now I'm caressing them, my hands gently touching these bread-and-spread snacks as if they're my father's fingers and mouth.

'Can I help you?'

A man in his thirties is manning the shop. I tell him that I'm just reminiscing about my father who'd have come here fifty-one years ago, on 15 September 1965, and would love to hear his memories of that day. The man sighs and shouts, 'Dad!' then goes out back to fetch him.

I wait eagerly for a few seconds, keen to gain an insight into what this journey must have been like for my father all those years ago. But when 'Dad' emerges, followed by his son, he's holding a rounders bat and wants to know if I'm the c-word who keeps 'robbing' the sandwiches and why.

I assure him I've never been here before, offer to leave and agree that no, I can't have some Lilt, and anyway it's 'stealing'. I leave with a flea in my ear, I don't mind saying! Still, I think as I jog off down the Norwich Road, good to paint a bit of colour on this sepia-tinted journey of yesteryear.

17.

I'M ONLY MAKING PLANS – FOR LIONEL

***

LIONEL GORDON PARTRIDGE WAS my father. In my opinion, he always will be, although there are some who argue that dads stop being your father once they're dead.

Born in April 1926, he grew up in that somewhat thick era after the Great War when people were saying, 'Well, we won't be doing that again!' only to do it again quite soon afterwards.

Little is known about his childhood, and Mother said it was only when he came back from the Second World War that his bad humour developed in earnest. I suggested many times that his grumpiness could be a very, very, very mild form of post-traumatic stress disorder, and that maybe he'd seen something awful like a fellow soldier get captured by drunken Germans and made to do a Morris dance while they laughed and shot at the ground near his feet. But both he and Mother insisted that this was absolute toffee.

I came along ten years after the war had ended, and what I do know is that he was a strong and fierce man, just like the Lion that makes up the first portion of his first name (Lionel). Yes, I was always impressed that his first name contained Lion. For he was always a Lion to me, his thick, black hair like a mane around his larger-than-average head. Plus he had a bad temper, which lions are also famous for.

One of my earliest memories? Standing on a pavement by a parade of shops while my mother attempted to parallel park again and again and again. We ended up shouting directions at the flustered woman, my father and I, until she got it right. I loved him that day.

Once a year, when he was drunk on Christmas sherry, I'd be allowed to clamber onto his back while he crawled around the room and pretended to paw at the lady guests in the room.

'Fatback the Lion!' I'd call him, and he'd tell me to shut it. 'This will happen to you when you hit forty,' he'd hiss. And sure enough, shortly after my fortieth birthday, I began to mushroom at the middle, gradually at first but then more noticeably, the lumbar area of my back happy to host a swathe of refugee fat displaced from more habitable parts of my body.[72] A parting gift from my father to me, and I very much hope I have passed this affliction on to my own son, Fernando.

I'm speculating again, but could it be that it was father's

given name that hardened him? 'Lionel' would have been an unusual name in East Anglia in the early half of the twentieth century, and he must surely have taken some stick for it. Stands to reason. There would, I imagine, have been lurid suggestions among the chortling children he grew up with that he was a practising homosexual, simply because he had a name that sounded light on its feet.

But this made my father teak-tough, and any physical confrontation between me and him would always end in his favour. Be it pinning me down, smacking my backside or just pushing me away when I'd become tiresome, he could summon the strength to overpower what by all accounts was a pretty active scout (me). Yes, it rankled, and yes, there were times when I'd fantasise about being big enough to turn around and thump him in the tummy or set fire to an Airfix Messerschmitt and put it behind his bedroom door so he'd be intoxicated by the burning plastic. But I sure as heck loved him.

Father struggled with my adolescence. Although we shared a house and took the odd foreign holiday as a family, he was a man of his time. And boy, was I a man of mine! Brash, confident, every bit one of the 'Children of the Revolution'

---

72 My own research suggests this hereditary complaint is a form of 'oestrogen dominance' combined with high insulin resistance, effectively meaning that anything containing carbs is going to set up shop just above the backside. Oestrogen dominance can occur in males and is more usually a cause of slack male tits. I'm fortunate that my chest is practically concave – moobs ain't no problem to me. Just, as I say, this unsightly fat back.

immortalised by Mark Bolam, I was a challenge to the status quo (as well as a fan of theirs). Father would have taken one look at my loose, long hair, flared denim trousers and pepper-pot brogues, and thought, 'Who the hell is this big-haired poof?'

Unfortunately, that BHP was me. And so it was that, after childhood, we didn't speak a great deal. I was almost forty when he died and I know it bothered him that he didn't live long enough to see me reach that milestone and develop a fat back, or long enough to find out whether Fernando had learning difficulties or was just unruly (just unruly).

But even though I've only been back to the graveyard in Sheringham where he lies on one occasion since his funeral (when interviewing an odd vicar for a high-quality documentary), I still find that within me he lives on.

I learned at my father's knee, and it's funny what rubs off on you. Like him, I instinctively station an arm behind the passenger-side headrest when reversing in the car. Like him, I don't like brassy waitresses who talk loudly and touch your shoulder. Like him, I adore sandwiches, although unlike him, I will eat other foods. And like him, I've become a touch snappier in later life.

I sometimes worry that growing older has mellowed my hatred of things, and with it my passion, my sharpness. But then a youth TV presenter says 'could of' instead of 'could have' and there I am throwing food at the television. My father used to do the same thing, although his food-hurling could be brought on by all manner of things he disliked. From something serious like the US government's handling of the Cuban Missile Crisis to something trivial like a black newscaster.

Yet despite these quirks we share, passed down from father to son like a collection of World Cup medals accrued from a petrol station via Esso's Tiger Token scheme, there is a disconnect. I feel like I never truly knew him. By pounding the streets from Norwich to Dungeness, I know that will change. I know it will. Because it will, I know it.

18.

COUNTY BORDERS

***

ABSOLUTELY FASCINATING CHAT WITH this morning's FedEx driver. He came to collect my rucksack from the B&B I was staying at in Manningtree, a poky little place staffed by a portly little family just off Quay Street. TripAdvice: their towels smell of mince.

Still! I'd slept well, and I was in good cheer as the driver came to collect my rucksack. We exchanged pleasantries, I asked about van driving, he asked about my walk. And I explained that I was using his company's services to ferry my bag onwards each day, an ingenious form of kick and chase. He frowned a little and we had a brief chat about costs, and – to cut a long story down a bit – he explained that doing this every day would cost me close to £900 over the course of the walk, money I just don't have. Or rather I do have, it's just not liquid right now.

So I sent him on his way and am now carrying my bags again, which in a daft kind of way I prefer. I thank my lucky stars I told my assistant to buy the most expensive ruckie she could find. Peace of mind!

Manningtree sits slap bang on the border between Suffolk and Essex. 'A new dawn, a new county,' I say out loud as I begin to walk. And though crossing a county border is always a thrilling experience, I feel sad to leave Suffolk behind. There's a lot of twaddle spoken about the rivalry between Suffolk and my own county, Norfolk. But I don't buy into it. Our real enemies are those counties further afield with designs on our loyal band of repeat-visit tourists. Your Devons, your Cumbrias, your Northumberlands, your Waleses.

It is they who spread rumours about us. Not least – and let's confront this head on because it's the elephant in the room – inbreeding. I have lived in East Anglia for over half a century and I have never – *never* – been made aware of, witnessed or been involved in so much as a single act of human inbreeding. When it comes to allowing the gene pool to stagnate, we simply do not have a charge to answer.

All right, you might say, it doesn't happen now, but it used to. And fair enough, it did used to. But what people fail to recognise is that East Anglia is in a remote part of the country. There's very little passing traffic there. So in centuries gone by, before technological advances such as the motor car or Tinder made it easy for people to make more genetically advisable choices, it was inevitable that on a cold winter's night, when everyone else in the house was asleep, a randy brother might walk down the corridor and gently knock on his sister's door.

No, if you ask me, I say let all the peoples of East Anglia come together to fight this threat from rival counties as one. Because it's together – by doctoring their Wikipedia entries, by leaving negative TripAdvisor reviews for hotels we haven't visited – that we can ensure our homeland retains its reputation as one of the world's premier destinations for competitively priced caravanning breaks and (thanks to the Colman's empire) mustard holidays.

And I'd go further. Life in Suffolk is hard. So let's give our neighbours a break. I guess the most obvious option would be to subsume Suffolk into Norfolk. The new super-county 'Norfolk', a compound word made by taking the 'Nor' from Norfolk and the 'folk' from Suffolk, would seek to spread Norfolk's better educational standards and – let's not dodge this – slightly advanced culture to our newest members. And with the name 'Suffolk' consigned to the history books (before being quietly removed altogether in future editions), maybe, just maybe, our disadvantaged neighbours would have a fighting chance of a better future.

***

To give me energy for the day ahead, I have prepared my own take on the glucose sachets now favoured by endurance athletes and bin men with particularly long rounds. A far cry from the overpriced equivalents of the big brands, mine comprise of a spoonful of jam tightly bound in cling film.

Whenever my performance starts to flag, I will just place one of the pellets – known colloquially as 'jam bombs' – into my mouth. As I bite down, the jam bomb – not to be confused with the French word *jambon*, meaning 'ham' – will detonate, its payload of thick fruit plasma oozing onto my tongue and into the mouth or mouths of my grateful taste buds – '*Cheers, Al! Love your radio show, by the way.*'

If my calculations are correct, I'll then feel a brief high, followed by a sustained period of extra energy. When the slump comes – and it will come – I'll simply repeat and continue. Some sports scientists believe this kind of short-term 'jam dosing' is bad for your health. Then again, sports scientists say a lot of things. It doesn't make them right. How much *actual* science is involved in being a sports scientist anyway? I mean them no disrespect but they're PE teachers with laptops.

I have breakfasted well on porridge and eggs (not in same bowl), so I know it will be some time before I need to turn to one of my small sugary assistants. And so it proves, my mouth not triggering the first controlled explosion until I've been on the road for fully forty minutes. And then . . .

Ka-boom!

I'm taken aback by how much better I feel and make a mental note to set up a call with the head of British Athletics. With top athletes constantly searching for even the most marginal gains, it's pretty obvious to me that jam, a product not yet on the World Anti-Doping Agency's list of banned substances, could be of serious interest to Team GB, or to be grammatically accurate, GB's team.

With one bomb consumed, I quickly find myself reaching for the next. In an ideal world they'd be taken on an 'as and when needed' basis, but because they're one of the nicest things ever made, this is impossible. I want to stop, *need* to stop, but stop I cannot. Within fifteen minutes the jam is no more. All that remains is a mouthful of spent cling film pieces and a nagging sense of self-loathing.

And then, the crash. The tiredness is overwhelming. I feel like a gorilla that's been shot with a tranquilliser dart or is just *extremely* tired. I try to power through it, but I'm being naive.

'Alan, you're being naive,' I say out loud. But I'm so exhausted it just comes out as, 'Ar ya bee nyee,' accompanied by some dribble.

Every step is like wading through, I dunno, treacle? Fybogel? Basically, it's *very* hard. I stagger into a home of God – the church of St Andrew in the village of Marks Tey – and make my way to a pew at the front. There's a service going on but that's not my concern right now, and it's not something that bothers me. I lie down, tell the vicar to shush, and fall soundly asleep.

Twenty minutes later, I wake with a scream (a recurring nightmare about petrol prices), bid farewell to the congregation and get on my way. Left, right, left, right, left, right. That's not my legs, by the way, it's my arms. It sounds weird, but my legs are actually doing the opposite – right, left, right, left, right, left – and the combination of the two somehow leads to the act of walking (*see fig. 1*).

POINT IN JOURNEY	STEP 1	STEP 2	STEP 3	STEP 4	STEP 5	STEP 6
FORWARD LEG	RIGHT	LEFT	RIGHT	LEFT	RIGHT	LEFT
FORWARD ARM	LEFT	RIGHT	LEFT	RIGHT	LEFT	RIGHT

Fig. 1 – Tabulation of traditional walking motion

© Peartree Infographics 2016

Like the old parlour game of patting your head while rubbing your balls, walking requires a real feat of co-ordination. I try not to overthink it. A boy at Cubs once told me that if you focus too hard on something that's confusing, you go insane. It's a fate I'm keen to avoid.

As I head towards the district of Braintree, I begin to muse on the word 'Braintree'. You can imagine it, can't you? A brain tree. Like an apple tree except instead of apples it bears human brains. I could think of a few broadcasters who could do with one of them in their garden! And yes, that amusing thought sustains me for a short time, helping to keep my ragged mind off the pain of walking. Of course it did, it's a funny thought. But is it going to make you laugh for any more than, what, twenty or twenty-five minutes? Probably not. And yes, you can muster additional laughs by thinking up variants on the 'brain tree' theme: I imagine there are towns called Spleenbush, Lungshrub, Bowelplant, etc., etc., and picture what the corresponding plants would look like. Funny, sure. And great – you've bought yourself another twenty minutes of amusement. But beyond that?

No, I could feel my spirits slumping. Perhaps I had bitten off more walk than I could chew.

I snap myself out of it to notice I'm approaching Braintree. Is it me or is there a feeling of anticipation in the air? The man walking a dog, the boy riding a bike, the lady driving a tractor (I genuinely did see this!) – do they seem somehow . . . expectant?

I start to see dribs and drabs of people standing by the side of the road. Four women on the left (a drib), two teens on the right (a drab). Soon the lines of people are thickening like a lorry driver's arteries. What's going on here today? A marathon, perhaps? An LGBT parade? A marathon's probably more likely given the part of the world we're in, but either way I feel a huge sense of relief that the crowds are not here for Alan Partridge.

Let me be clear: this walk is not about me. And the very suggestion that I might have dreamed it all up with one eye on a spin-off range of high-quality yet affordable merchandise featuring Alan Partridge hiking socks, bivvy bags, jerry cans and flints is actually quite offensive.

No, dear reader, we'll leave that kind of ugly careerism to the likes of Tony Robinson (Channel 4's *Walking Through History*) and John Inverdale (Channel 5's *Feel the Power*, a speed-boating series in which John drives dead fast across the Solent with no top on. This one wasn't actually commissioned, but I know for a fact that Inverdale pitched it, so my point still stands).

My reasons for doing this walk are intensely personal (i.e. footsteps of father). And much though I sense the crowd would love it, that doesn't mean signing autographs or posing for 'selfers'. I put on my headphones, crank my iPhone up to full blast and nod approvingly.

'Dr Alban,' I say to myself. 'Spot on.'

It's crucial for a rambler to get their song choice right. I live alone, so often find myself marching back and forth to pop songs. 'Stop the Cavalry' by Jona Lewie, 'Portsmouth' by Mike Oldfield and 'The Safety Dance' by Men Without Hats all lend themselves to a brisk hup-two-three-four, but as marching songs go, you cannot beat 'Float On' by Modest Mouse (a 2004 track I heard at an ice rink), because the singer sounds like Bryan Ferry, whom I know from Tory party fundraisers.

Time was, I would have plumped for 'Danger Zone' by Kenny Loggins. On long drives, my friend Eammon Holmes and I would play the *Top Gun* soundtrack at high volume. One would pretend to be Maverick, the other Goose (take it in turns), and we'd don Ray-Bans, talk in American accents and keep saying we were 'the best of the best'. But I can't listen to this song now. Not for any painful memories; it's just a terrible piece of music.

No, Alban it must be, and Allbran it is.

With the Doctor's distinctive Afro-European beats coursing through my veins, blocking out the crowds is a breeze. Admittedly, I do wave at them occasionally, but that's primarily a health and safety thing to ensure they don't get in my way. And while my moonwalk does elicit a cheer, I only really do it to relieve cramp in the soles of my feet.

But then something occurs to me. Maybe I've got this all wrong. I'm not saying this *is* the case, but what if these crowds are for me? Let's consider the facts. There are no marathon runners. There are no floats with flamboyant homosexuals in outrageous costumes (I *love* those guys). But there is an Alan Partridge. *I* didn't set out to publicise my walk, but what if someone else did?

For many years Dave Clifton was my arch-enemy, and in the late nineties and early noughties not a day went by when I didn't wish him dead. In more recent times, however, we've buried the hatchet. We don't go drinking together because Dave's a big-time sauce junky, and we don't go for meals together because that would be weird, but I do know that he now considers me a friend.[73] He also happens to be filling in for me on *Mid Morning Matters*. Yes, there's every possibility these crowds are his doing.

(Dave, you're a good man. Whatever people say, you're a good, good man. *Stay sober.*)

Well, I hardly need tell you, this is most unexpected. But I'll be honest, it feels good. All the naysayers, the doubters, the sniffers, the tutters (and that's just the staff of North Norfolk Digital!) must now surely be opening their mouths wide, dislocating their jaws and praying their gag reflex isn't too trigger-happy – as they now swallow their words. With everything now clear, I feel a smile beginning to form in and around the curls of my mouth.

I wave. Two girls wave back. I wink at some chaps. The chaps fire back a thumbs up (each). I raise my arms and wave the wave of a guy who lands planes. And that too is met in kind.

Yeah, I think. You love this, dontcha! I do a little jog and pretend to play an imaginary cricket stroke into the crowd

---

73 Indeed, he texted me last month with a message that simply said, 'You are my friend.' Odd.

then cap it off with a laugh and a get-outta-here wave. Then I do a series of rapid points at various members of the crowd – while mouthing, 'You, you, you, you, you,' before shouting, 'Who loves ya, baby!' I feel light on my feet, buoyant, cock of the frigging walk. I stand, hands on hips, letting them admire my stance, body and confidence. Then I'm off again, a little showbiz jog to the side, before leaning one way and cupping a hand to my ear. And then the other side. Jog, lean, cup. And now I'm striding down the highway, my hands above my head, spanking each other rhythmically to the drumbeat Roger Taylor designed for Queen's pop song 'We Will Rock You'. Dum, dum, chick. Dum, dum, chick.

I sometimes have a bit of a downer on the general public – they can be thick and uncultured[74] – but not this lot. This lot are amazing. I feel like I wanna give them something to say thanks. A memento of some kind.

I once saw a tennis player throw his sweatbands into the stands after a victory, and while I thought it was disgusting and wanted to be sick, his fans seemed to love it. I don't have any sweatbands, so I rummage around in my backpack to find a few things I can throw. As I ransack the rucksack, I see a banner. Held aloft by two housewives wearing a lot of denim, it clearly bears the Sport Relief logo.

Yep, thought this might happen, I think as I rifle through my bag. A lot of celebrities volunteer their time for Sport Relief and my CV makes me just the kind of person they might ask to complete a televised endurance event for

---

74 e.g. *The Great British Bake Off.*

faraway orphans. This particular year the organisers didn't come calling – they're busy people and you can't expect them to reply to every letter – but I'm happy to make that clear.

'I'm not doing it for Sport Relief,' I say, really rooting in the depths of my sack. 'So you might want to remove the banner.'

'Eh?' chirp the denim girls, in unison. That's literally what they said. But then this is Essex, and I'm aware they might not have had the benefit of a formal education. I smile and respond in a friendly manner, still searching for items to give away to the well-wishers.

'Get rid of the banner. Now.'

I look down again. Ah, good. Clothes. And I stand up, ready to hurl a memento into the crowd.

'But he'll be here in a minute,' they reply, again in annoying unison. I'd assumed they were identical twins but one of them's black.

'Who?' I say as I pull my arm back, ready to launch a pair of my underpants high into the sky for a lucky punter to keep. And that's when I notice that there isn't just one Sport Relief banner. There are loads of them. In fact, all over the place I now see people carrying Sport Relief collection buckets.

'Steve Backshall.'

The words hit me just as my arm completes its journey. Before I can register what this means, the scrunts have been flung. And as I watch them arc into a group of unsuspecting spectators, I grasp what this means. These people aren't here for me.

They're here to support a Sport Relief walk being done by Steve Backshall. And I, Alan Partridge, am effectively shelling them with unders. I wince and feel the tentacles of embarrassment beginning to climb my tummy like ivy.

For those of you who don't know him, and I have to admit I'm not massively familiar with the guy myself, Steve Backshall (pronounced 'back shawl') is a TV presenter who makes animal programmes for kids. His USP is that he films in exotic, often dangerous jungle locations. And while no shoot would ever be allowed to take place without a rigorous risk assessment that reduces the chances of anything going wrong to more or less zero, I've no doubt the shows appear extremely impressive, especially to the children at whom they are aimed.

But despite the attraction of having a surname that sounds like a knitted garment worn by a grandma, Back-shawl's core audience can only take him so far. Marooned in the no man's land between Bear Grylls and Terry Nutkins, his career has hit a glass ceiling.

Finding out that Backshall is due to arrive any minute, I decide to leave. Steve's a young fella trying to make his way in broadcasting, and even though it's not something that particularly bothers *me*, I can imagine how important the adulation of these people is to his self-esteem. The last thing he needs is an 800-pound gorilla stealing his thunder.

I do track down the organisers and give them my number – as the senior broadcaster I'd be happy for Steve to call if he needs any advice on how to handle the media, how to grow his brand or indeed how to knock some of the rough edges off his presenting style[75] – but with that done, it's time to get on my way. I make a quick foray into the crowd to collect my undies – 'Sorry, thanks, sorry, bye' – have a quick altercation with a middle-aged woman,[76] and continue south.

---

75 Like I say, I don't particularly follow his career but I know Steve does have a tendency to be a bit squeaky when he's doing a piece to camera. It's probably just nerves.

76 The pants weren't 'dirty'; they were 'unwashed'. Big difference, sweetheart.

19.

RIVER CAN AND ALAN CAN

***

I SPENT LAST NIGHT in the Oakmore Guesthouse in Feering, where for £89 I got bed, breakfast and a wake-up call I hadn't asked for.

I have no issue with those who wish to rise at 4 a.m. What I do have an issue with is when those people (or in this case 'that blackbird') proceed to spend the next four hours hollering from the top of a tree. I'm well aware that males of all species are randy in the morning, and the blackbird is no exception. But surely his desire to make love to a lady bird (i.e. a female bird) has such a low chance of success at that time in the morning that he'd be better off flying down to ground level and finishing himself off in a bush.

And while I don't run through *all* of these details with the landlady over breakfast, I do suggest that since I've only had half a night's sleep perhaps she'd like to charge me half a night's rate. She doesn't go for this idea, but you see the thing is she's dug her own grave there because later today I'm going to absolutely rinse her on TripAdvisor.

***

Today is day six, Thursday, and I'm heading towards Chelmsford, home to the River Can, whose very name hums with positivity, just like I always do. I've now completed a third of my journey and my legs are stronger and bulkier than ever before, especially the left one.

My father would have reached here in about ninety mins, whereas it's taken me six days. But that's not the point. In fact, you could argue that the slower I go, the more I am honouring him. Also, today's cars are faster than in my father's day, so if I'd driven I'd have got to Dungeness in less time than he did, which would effectively be like mocking the dead or dancing on his grave.

The break of day has brung rain. Bucketloads, in fact. Which is kinda funny because in order to collect donations towards my charity of choice, I'm now *carrying* a bucket.

I don't remember if I mentioned I'd be raising money for the needy, but I am. It's something I had in mind long before yesterday's run-in with the Sport Relief mob. It just so happens that by a weird coincidence I chanced upon a rather lovely bucket shop this morning, and it seemed silly not to get one. (Technically, it was a Sainsbury's, but it did sell buckets so I'm still being accurate.)

I know there'll be a few idiots who suggest I'm just using charity to boost my profile, like a long list of other celebrity do-gooders, or did-gooders, not least Backshall, but like a fully functioning helicopter I'll simply rise above that.

As to the charity I'm supporting, well, I've given it careful consideration. After all, ours is a nation not lacking in good causes. There's Help the Aged and Barnardo's, and even charities for animals, supported by the growing number of people who haven't got their priorities right. Yet if you're truly going to throw your weight behind something, it's important you're passionate about it. Consider Help the Aged. Don't get me wrong, I have no axe to grind with (or at!) the elderly, but am I passionate about them? Of course I'm not. Why would I be?

Besides which, I am on a journey in the footsteps of my father, a journey that will take me all the way to Dungeness 'A' nuclear power station. I'd be letting myself down – no, I'd be letting *my father* down – if I failed to pick a charity that was relevant to this.

Founded in 2011, the Alvin Weinberg Foundation is the world's first pro-nuclear charity. With an ongoing mission to support the safe and sustainable use of nuclear energy, the foundation runs numerous advocacy campaigns and has a well-respected outreach programme. Unfortunately for me, however, its name doesn't fit on my bucket, so in the end I just go with 'Alvin's Foundation'.

And by lunchtime I've raised over £60 for a power source that will surely play a key role in our nation's future energy mix. I do admit to feeling a slight twinge of guilt, but that's only because some of that money might have been donated because people assumed Alvin was a little boy with leukaemia.

By 1 p.m. the weather system has put an end to my charitable endeavours. As the heavens open and the rain sheets down, I can't help but wonder if the environmental brigade have found out what I'm up to and performed a rain dance at Greenpeace HQ, no doubt accompanied by an Enya CD.

The London Container Terminal at Tilbury, Essex.

My visit to this world-leading facility was a real highlight of my journey, or would have been if I'd been granted entry. Instead I spent several blissed-out hours gazing over the fence at these gentle cuboid giants. Indeed it was the memory of these containers that recently inspired me to begin work on *Container Bear*, a charming children's story (illustrated by myself) about a bear who dreams of finding a better life by stowing away on a container ship bound for the London Container Terminal.

My assistant was concerned that this was a very similar set-up to *Paddington Bear*, but of course she was quite wrong. Paddington crossed the sea under the canvas of a ship's lifeboat and would have been more than able to breathe. My own hero, on the other hand – locked in an airtight container – would have had no such luck, passing away through suffocation soon after leaving port. Yet rather than posing a 'fundamental problem' for my story it proved to be its salvation, as I realised that the death of the bear would allow his ghost to emerge and become the real hero of *Container Bear*. It was a masterstroke and I'm delighted with how the book has turned out. (Interested publishers should contact my agent, quickly.)

I'm told that in London the 'hipsters' or 'trendlies' have taken to using old shipping containers as offices or retail spaces. A lot of people think this is 'cool' but in actual fact it's 'not'. These containers have earned the right to a dignified retirement. They have spent their lives in the service of commerce, criss-crossing the seven seas, often in perilous conditions. What have millennials ever done, apart from a bit of freelance graphic design work? Pathetic.

Gatwick Airport, the site of my largely successful run-in with Harvey Kennedy.

There can be little doubt that the continued stalling over airport expansion in the south-east of England is hurting British business and is actually quite boring. For what it's worth, Alan Partridge's view is that limiting the debate to Heathrow or Gatwick is wrong and that there's another hat that should be thrown into the ring. The hat of Norwich International Airport.

Situated just three hours from the centre of London (or less, if you drive faster), Norwich International Airport is ripe/quivering for expansion. And although locals wouldn't have much interest in daily non-stop flights to over fifty Chinese cities, the business leaders of the south-east would.

As with adding capacity to any airport there'd be opposition groups to deal with. But again, Norwich (or 'London Norwich' as the airport would be re-named) has an advantage over Gatwick and Heathrow. By dint of their public school educations, the people who live in and around the capital are loud, tech-savvy and often called Julian. To them, organising an effective protest movement on social media is easy. For the citizens of Norfolk on the other hand, it isn't. Sure we have our digital trail-blazers (Norfolk was one of the first counties to go live with an app allowing holidaymakers to check the availability of static caravan accommodation in real-time), but on the whole internet technology has yet to make an impression on people's lives. As a result, opposition would be minimal and it would be fairly easy to push through legislation to add, what, eight new runways to Norwich International Airport? It's a plan to which I say a definite 'ni hao'.

Nick Knowles, photographed by me after we'd co-presented the Norfolk Young Farmer of the Year award in 2009.

I asked if he was sure he wanted to keep his jacket buttons done up, to which he replied: 'What did you say?' in that cockney way where it's unclear if he hadn't heard or was daring me to repeat something that riled him. 'Actually forget it,' I said. 'No, no,' said Nick. 'What did you say?' I laughed. 'Seriously,' said Nick. 'What did you say?' 'Forget it,' I said but he was suddenly in my face. 'Tell me what you said'. This carried on for a while until I told him what I'd said and it turned out he'd genuinely just not heard so everything was fine.

The M20 Motorway.

A photograph of the M20, which I took while driving. The car in front was driving like an absolute tool, cutting in front of me so as to spray my windscreen with rainwater – a practice my friends and I call 'skunking'. I'd only undertaken the drive in the hope of finding a face towel I'd left on the hard shoulder during my walk, praying I'd spot it on the tarmac or snagged in bramble. If you regularly use the road and see my towel, please post it to my publishers. It's blue and says 'LA Fitness' on it. Similarly, if you found it and have been using it, simply launder the item and post it back to me (folded) to avoid further action.

Pebble with white circle.

I found this pebble on the second day of my journey and it came to mean a great deal to me. It's heavier than you'd think and resembles a fossilised fish eye. But I don't mind that. I found it on the front door step of a semi-detached house. It was just lying there, next to a small collection of sticks and other interesting pebbles. They clearly belonged to a small child or a grown up with learning difficulties, but I didn't feel bad about stealing this one because I liked it and I wanted to have it. I still have the stone to this day. It lies on my front door step in the hope that one day its rightful owner will pass by my house and spot it. At which point I will happily regale them with stories of the journey it has been on and return it to them in exchange for a small fee (£20).

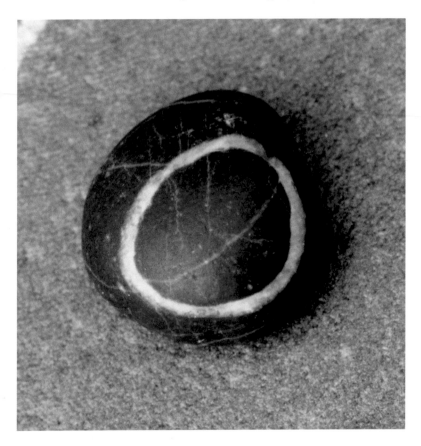

The William Harvey Hospital, Ashford.

There's not a great deal you can say about a hospital, especially one in which you were heavily sedated, but I'm contractually obliged to provide a caption for every photo and I'm happy to honour that. One thing I fondly remember is that when you approach the hospital (which is part of the NHS and East Kent Hospitals NHS Trust), the Accident and Emergency ward is straight ahead of you and, if memory serves, so is the Out-Patients Drop-Off Point. If it's the Channel Day Surgery and Car Park you're after, be sure to go straight on, while visitors for the Rotary Suite and Car Park should also head in a straight-onwardly direction. I distinctly recall that the hospital has a visitors car park but to get to it, you needed to head left where you could enjoy disabled parking and parking alike. I've just remembered another thing which is that there's a 'renal services' at the hospital but to locate it, you need to be heading away from the car park – so right as you head up the road. Different directions for different things then, a bit like life!

The entrance to the Channel Tunnel. (*Opposite page*)

The Channel Tunnel: a glorified pipe that, at the time of my visit, was a welcome conduit to our continental friends. Since then, Britain has voted to leave Europe. It's chilling to think that had I entered this tunnel after the referendum, I'd have been seized by European border guards and slung into a detention centre, my wrists bound by the very red tape that the bloated institution of the EU or EC or Eurozone, or whatever it is, produces obsessively.

Dungeness A Nuclear Power Station, photographed – as all nuclear power plants should be – on a sunny day.

Viewed like this, in glorious sunshine with the sea shimmering in the background, it's hard to imagine the station being anything other than a clean and safe provider of energy for generations to come. So it's a shame that green activists will tamper with the picture to include a child on the beach, just visible in the distance, her tiny webbed hand holding a single balloon, thereby making a perfectly pleasant vision of Britain's nuclear future horribly sinister.

A dead chap I know called Michael.

I never took a photograph of Michael because he found flashes frightening and I don't know how to turn the flash off on my cell phone, but a therapist suggested I might like to draw him and she was right – I did. Borrowing the ID mugshot from his security lanyard, I spent two evenings sketching his face, and am proud/happy with the results, with this being the strongest and most moving of my six attempts. Note the brave smile common among PTSD sufferers, the military buzzcut designed to prevent lice infestations and my decision not to include the broken capillaries since they looked like blood fireworks going off under his skin. But it's the eyes that really clinch it. My therapist said his eyes seem to follow you around the room and I'm thrilled to have captured that, because it's something they used to do to women in real life, especially if he was drunk.

20.

TILBURY AND THE BLOOD OF MY HEEL

***

FRIDAY IS DAY SEVEN and something of a red-letter day as I reach the banks – but not the building societies! – of the River Thames at Tilbury. It's a major milestone in my journey and I celebrate in fine style with a pack of wafer-thin ham from Asda.

Admittedly, it's a moment that would have had more significance if my father had passed this way, but there's no road crossing here so he would have used the Dartford Tunnel a few clicks west. As for me, well, I had to come this way because Tilbury is home to one of Britain's largest shipping container terminals, and it would have been a bit weird of me not to take a look.

Tilbury is also one of the most ancient ports on the Thames. A fort was built here by Henry VIII. It's where Queen Elizabeth I once came ashore to inspect her army. And it's even believed to have been the site of a Roman settlement. But as I say, I'm not really bothered about that stuff. I'm more interested in the London Container Terminal, for as well as handling a variety of bulk cargo, mainly timber and cars, the terminal is also the main UK hub for importing paper.

I ask the man at the gate if they do tours. He says they don't. I ask the man at the gate if they do tours for VIPs. He says they don't. I ask the man at the gate if they do tours for VIPs who will keep out of everyone's way and promise not to be a nuisance. He says they don't.

It's fun to stand over the road and watch the terminal at work, my mind afizz with images of timber and cars and paper. I love the sense of mystery. What treasure lies within each container? Is it timber? Is it cars? Is it paper?

As I marvel at the sophistication of the computer-controlled crane system stacking the containers, I have a vivid sense of how the world will be when the robots take over in about twenty years' time. Bill thinks it will take longer – this is Bill Oddie by the way, he's been with me all day – but he's wrong about this one and I think he knows it.

It's good to have Bill with me. It's the kind of comfortable friendship where both parties can happily share a silence. And we do, for the best part of three hours, so that it becomes increasingly unclear whether we're *sharing* a silence or I am just putting up with Bill's. It may very well be that I'd cast him into a sulk when I said seagulls were the 'jackals of the sky'. I don't even know what I meant by it, but I saw his cheek twitch and I think that was the last thing either of us said.

As we head to the ferry port to take the short crossing over to Gravesend, Bill gets a text on the 'birdphone', the mobile he keeps exclusively for alerts on rare bird sightings. Someone's just spotted a White-crowned Sparrow in Dorset, and I am sorely mistaken if I think he's going to miss that. He calls an Uber, and before I can say boo to a goose – not that I would when Bill's around – the diminutive birdaholic has packed himself off in a Dorset-bound cab that will cost him £200 I know he doesn't have.

Fare thee well, old friend, with your 'noculars[77] and your jerkin of a thousand pockets. May the avian gods smile down on you this day, and all days.

***

When walking I often like to pretend I'm a car. Listen carefully when you cycle past me on a straight bit of road and you'll most likely hear me making the noise of a family saloon accelerating. And with Oddie Time now over, my imaginary car of choice is a Vauxhall Cascada. Obviously I'd never drive one in real life as it's a bit of a hairdresser's car, but in the land of make-believe no such stigma applies.

I'm looking for the ferry, and as I negotiate a corner by making the sound of the Cascada dropping down a couple of gears, I notice a van bearing the distinctive livery of the BBC. It's an Outside Broadcast Unit, and standing next to

---

77 Poetic abbreviation of 'binoculars'.

it is none other than CBBC's Steve Backshall. It's 7 p.m., so most of his supporters have been taken home by their mums, but Steve – ever keen to raise his own profile – is about to do an interview with the BBC's neither-one-thing-nor-the-other programme *The One Show*, so-called because that's how many brain cells you need to watch it.[78]

As they go on air I'm delighted to see that the interviewer is Gyles Brandreth. Now, I love Gyles. A lot of people think he's just a privileged posh boy, but I've researched him on Wikipedia and other than founding a teddy bear museum in 1998, which admittedly is a bit odd, Brandreth could hardly be more normal. Yet just because he went to private school, took to wearing a cape when at Oxford and his middle name is Daubeney, people suddenly think they can make judgements about him. Well, it's not on. I know loads of people called Daubeney. Who doesn't?

As I eat the last of my Asda ham, I watch the two men talk. Gyles is, as ever, a class act – a raised eyebrow here, a touch on the arm there, a kindly nod while Backshall drones on – betraying not a jot of the contempt he must surely hold for the programme that employs him.

But my eye is drawn to Backshall. His wide-eyed expression, his constant references to all the money he's raised, his cloying self-satisfaction and his laughter. Oh, the guy can't stop laughing. He's laughing right now. It seems that in Backshallworld, everything is funny. Beaming and laughing and smiling and laughing and talking and laughing and fundraising and laughing and being Steve Backshall and

---

78 Eamonn Holmes gave me that one. Love you, Eam!

laughing. I watch all of this spewing from his mouth like the suds from a cartoon washing machine gone haywire. He's so *pleased* with himself. You'd think no one else was doing a walk. Well, they are. Me.

And with that, a thought suddenly erupts in my mind like one of those geysers that smell of trumps.[79] Since my journey began I've been doing my best to *avoid* the spotlight. But maybe I've got things anus about chest.[80] The more I chew it over, the more I think that my father's memory shouldn't be hidden from view like some sausages in a fridge. We live in the age of sharing – LinkedUp, Instagran and the like. If it's fair game to tell the whole world when you last took toilet or what you had for breakfast – perhaps sausages from the fridge – then surely it's only right that I should share the memory of the man who made me. And if it's fair game for Backshall to speak to the British public on the flagship chit-chat magazine show, then it's surely only right for Partridge to peck on that pie too. It's one interview! Big deal. It's not like I'm making a six-part Sunday night BBC One series about it. That ship has sailed. I'm fine with it. Move on.

I jog over and thrust my hand towards Steve, calmly ignoring the producer's frantic gestures telling me to keep back.

'Alan Partridge. I don't believe we've had the pleasure.' I put the emphasis on pleasure so that we all know I mean the opposite.

---

79 It's at this moment that I realise I have actually trumped, an unpleasant habit I am working hard towards eradicating.
80 Arse about tit.

As our hands lock and we begin the traditional up-and-down greeting action, I quickly realise his shake is way firmer than mine. I try to get up to his level without him realising but end up gritting my teeth and I think he notices. Off-camera, the producer's still going bananas and some of the stuff he's miming at me is actually pretty industrial. If this was *Give Us a Clue* almost all of it would have to be cut, as I believe a lot of Lionel Blair's stuff was in the later years, when he became increasingly blue. But Brandreth knows me – we once rehearsed a panto together, although my part, Twanky's Friend, was subsequently cut before opening night – and he welcomes me warmly. I start chatting and tell Gyles (and the viewers) that I'm also doing a walk.

'How splendid,' says Gyles.

Now, there aren't many broadcasters who'd think to use a word like 'splendid' on primetime TV. But I guess that's part of Gyles's gift. He goes on: 'You and Steve are both in the midst of walks. But whereas your feet are shod, Steve's are – how to put this? – *al fresco.*'

Al fresco. Again, brilliant. I have no idea what he means but it's still quite, quite brilliant. Then I realise. Backshall has nothing on his feet. He's doing his Sport Relief walk with no shoes on. Of course! Sport Relief requires its annual celebrity to add a twist to the feat of endurance – be it asking David Williams to swim open-mouthed into sewage or getting Eddie Izzard to drive 100 marathons in 100 days – and this is Backshall's angle: Zola Budding it around the place like a wally.

'Wowzers,' I say.

I'm pretending to be impressed but the arrogance staggers

me. And I think it staggers Gyles too. Who walks without shoes on? Who does he think he is, John Lennon from the Beatles? Then again . . . it does sound kinda fun.

'You know what, Steve? I'm going to walk with mine off too!'

Well, I can almost *hear* the gasps. This is *great* TV. You'd think I'd be a bit rusty, having not been live in front of the nation for years, but I have come alive. Adrenaline's flying round my body like it used to when Angela said she'd made one of her chicken pies.[81]

By now my shoes and socks are off, I've decided to roll up my trousers and I'm hopping from foot to foot like a madman.

'Oh no, my feet haven't got any clothes on!'

What *do* I look like? I bet the viewers at home are killing themselves at this.

'Call the cops, call the cops! My feet need to get arrested for indecent exposure!'

I've got to hand it to Gyles, how on *earth* he isn't corpsing I have no idea. Steve's blank expression is less surprising. Kids' TV presenters tend to have a kid's sense of humour, so this stuff is probably going straight over his head.

Of course, little do they know that I have an ulterior motive. This isn't just some surreal outburst of physical comedy that bears comparison with the best of *The Goon Show*. I mean it is that, but it's also something else. It's not often one gets a platform like this, and while Backshall may be standing there like a pudding, I have seen the opportunity

---

81 Call me. Please.

to tell people about my walk. And it's an opportunity I intend to seize with both feet.

My calculations are simple. With my side-to-side jumping becoming increasingly frantic, people will be unable to take their eyes off me. In the fifteen or so seconds before I become exhausted and have to stop for a nap, I'll outline the significance of my journey, list the towns I'll be passing through in the coming days and recommend some spots to grab a bite to eat along the way – just quote the word 'footsteps' when making your booking for 10 per cent off the bill, offer does not include alcohol.

It promises to be a mesmerising piece of infotainment, and I can't help but snigger at how I'm about to totally 'own' Steve Backshall.

'So, we've all heard about Steve's walk . . .' I mime a large yawning gesture, and although Gyles doesn't laugh I can tell he wants to. 'Well, now let's hear about m— OW!!!'

Glass. That was glass. I have trodden on glass.

***

I'm surprised at just how much blood a heel contains. Then again, if blood is going to gather anywhere, it stands to reason it should be in the feet. I take off, wheeling around the car park like a spooked horse on its period (what a *horrible* image). Unaware that it's only a small cut, my first thoughts turn to crisis management. I scream at the top of my voice, 'Tell the BBC they're sending me private! There's no way I'm using the NHS.'

'It's OK,' replies Brandreth as I complete my third circuit of the car park. 'I'm sure they'll "foot" the bill.'

What an absolute A-hole. I vow there and then never to watch another episode of *Countdown*.

And, shag a dog, it *had* to be my left, didn't it? Ignore the film of the same name, because *My* Left Foot is the real story here. Several years ago I pierced this foot on a spike while hurdling some railings to rescue a corporate function. (After a series of operations and a dozen Paul McKenna hypnotherapy sessions,[82] the foot finally stopped aching.) Then, a few years ago, I was shot in the left ankle by a madman's shotgun. And now this gash. (The gunshot wound, by the way, hurt like billy-o and I've only just stopped telling people about it. Although I shall now start telling people about it again as this will allow me to complete the following chapter.)

---

82 What absolute bollocks that was.

21.

'YOU DON'T HAVE TO BE MAD TO WORK HERE . . . BUT PAT WAS!'

***

PEOPLE OFTEN ASK ME why I veer to the right on long walks. My answer is always the same. It's a bit of gyp around my left ankle that flares up when I walk, a small 'hello' from my body's nerve centre to me, like a 'poke' from a divorcee you've not Facebooked for a while.

The source of the pain? A small fragment of shotgun pellet lodged next to the tibia and, according to the lady surgeon who delved into me, nothing to worry about whatsoever. The decision was made to leave the fragment in my body, and it's something I enjoy telling people about – whenever I possibly can.

Because it came from the barrel of a madman's shotgun

and it changed the way I look at *everything*.[83] Even though the shot wasn't fatal, Alan Partridge died that day. And a new Alan Partridge was born. A wiser, cooler, kinder Partridge. A Partridge I've become rather fond of.[84]

To understand more, let me take you back to the summer of 2013. Q3 '13 was an odd time for Alan Partridge, a period of flux, as evidenced by the daring hair style I'd developed – a slightly looser, longer, loucher, lanker style. You're never too old to experiment! Although you wouldn't know it from the outraged response when I presented it to the world. 'I don't understand why your hair is like that,' people would say, like it even frigging mattered. 'You don't even look like Alan anymore. Why is it like that? That's not Alan. Alan's is shorter. Why have you made it long at the back? It shouldn't be long. Alan has short hair.'

Yes, just as I changed into a different Alan Partridge through the use of a cool new hairdo, so it was that change almost led to tragedy – although mercifully no one was hurt (with the exception of Michael, who died). I guess you could say that change is the theme of this chapter.

---

83 Not everything.

84 For one thing, it gave me a new perspective on the killing of Forbes McAllister, a death that has weighed heavy on me, on and off, for three decades. Forbes, you'll remember, was tragically shot on the (as it turned out) final episode of my television chat show. Now I too have been shot. We've essentially been through the same thing. And while my family didn't get lawyers involved and start pointing fingers at Farrell and crying outside tribunals, that may just be because I come from nicer stock. It may also be because Farrell didn't pull the trigger (can't remember who did).

***

As Sheryl Crow once squawked: 'A change . . .[85] would do you good.[86] I think a change . . .[87] would do you good.[88] Oh, I think a change . . .[89] would do you good.'[90]

And change *can* do good. But only if managed correctly. Change is one of the most powerful forces known to science – be it small change like a caterpillar getting changed in a chrysalis, to large change like a menopausing woman. Yep, change is hard to resist. But whether you believe in evolution or revolution (or devolution), you can't go in blunderhanded. Because *badly managed* change, OK, can blow up in your face.

[Pause.[91]]

It's a shame a company called Gordale Media didn't consider any of this when they rode into town back in 2013.

I'd had concerns about the strategic direction of North Norfolk Digital for some time. The 10 a.m. to 2 p.m. weekday slot seemed to be the only segment of the station's output that wasn't either horrendously conceived or appallingly executed – or, in the case of Danny Sinclair's *Breakfast Show*,

---

85 Backing singer: 'A change would do you good!'

86 Backing singer: 'A change would do you good!'

87 Backing singer: 'A change would do you good!'

88 Backing singer: 'A change would do you good!'

89 Backing singer: 'A change would do you good!'

90 Backing singer: 'A change would do you good!'

91 I should point out that these opening paragraphs were lifted directly from a TED talk I wrote but was subsequently not required to give.

both. And that's not me having a go at my fellow DJs. That's just analysis.

I knew my onions. Don't forget, I'd created Forward Solutions, a unique business-training programme endorsed by none other than Chip Keeble,[92] so I was able to assess businesses with a clinical eye and a surgical ear.

Within minutes of striding into *any* office or shop, I was (and am) able to identify failing processes, dream up an attitude matrix, suggest mantras that management must repeat to staff each morning and generally map out a roadpath to collective betterment. And all without the mumbo jumbo you often get from management consultants.

And that's why I had offered to come into North Norfolk Digital with a package of evening workshops, hosted by me at a discounted rate, which would 'revolitalise' (my word) the ailing station. My methodology was by now pretty watertight. Once everyone had kicked off their shoes and limbered up, I'd ask the group to debate among themselves and divide up into heroes (the emphasis was very much on positive change, remember) and cancers. The cancers were then asked to leave the station permanently (I called this the democratisation of dismissal) and the remainder would get to continue working there, with the proviso that they adopt a set of non-negotiable recommendations relating to their future conduct.

Yes, it was tough love. But I'd been shown a film called *Glen Garryglen Ross* – basically a movie version of *The*

---

92 Who is American.

Apprentice – and it had increased my toughness by a factor of two. I was convinced it would turn North Norfolk Digital into a viable, robust and agile twenty-first century business. Unfortunately, the powers that be felt they knew best and declined my offer.

So you'll forgive me if my gast wasn't exactly flabbered[93] when, six months later, Gordale Media, the station's new owners, sought to make a few changes of their own and the whole place kicked off big time.

A radio station is a piece of precision engineering. It's like a Swiss watch or a Segway. Its equilibrium is delicate. You can't remove a cog here or a wheel there or a DJ over there without causing a few shockwaves. It's like chaos theory. If a butterfly flaps its wings in the boardroom, an Irishman's gonna go berserk in Studio 2.

And that is exactly what happened, with the exception of the butterfly bit, which didn't. (The closest North Norfolk Digital has ever had to its own butterfly was a moth infestation above a ceiling tile in the women's toilets.)

The Irishman in question was Pat Farrell, whose weekday evening show *Roll Out the Farrell* had been a feature of the station's output for years, in the same way a benign mole is a feature of a woman's back: it's not a problem per se but you'd rather it wasn't there. Or at least that was the prevailing view. Personally, I had no beef with Pat and would

---

93 This was a phrase first used by Paul Ross in 1990 that I have always found deliciously clever.

have loved for him to stay. It was the bosses who wanted to get rid of him. I even volunteered to stand up for Pat at a meeting of the company's top brass, but when I got to the boardroom the door was jammed so I couldn't get in. All I heard was them mumbling about Pat's union activities and his foul mouth. I was desperate to make them see sense. 'Just save Pat! For God's sake!' I wanted to say. But the door had other ideas and stayed jammed. There was nothing I could do but walk away from the jammed door.

Later that day, Pat was dismissed. I wanted to console him but I could tell from his body language that he wanted to be alone.

As Pat strode from the building to the snarky sniggers of his former friends, I stood alone, with a sense of unease. Something about his expression said to me he wasn't going to take this lying down. I knew there and then that he was a security threat and we all needed to be on our guard(s). But the others were too busy sniggering to heed my misgivings.

'Oh come on, Alan. Why aren't you sniggering?' said one.

'We're all sniggering, why aren't you?' said another.

'Why don't you snigger for a bit with us?' said a third.

'Nah,' I said, my eyes still trained on the door. 'You guys snigger without me. I gotta check something out.' I looked at them, smiled wryly and jogged off.

***

Minutes later, I was in the office of station manager Greg Frampton, pleading with him to beef up security ahead of that night's party.[94] But Greg wasn't listening. Nor were any of the management team when I raised the issue with them. And that's where I left it.

And that eats me up. Maybe I should have done more, said more, shouted more, slapped the desk more. Maybe I should have trashed the place and forced the postponement of the party by reason of a capsized buffet table. But I didn't. And God, that's hard for me to live with. I'm just thankful that no one was hurt (with the exception of Michael, who died).

Because little did my cackling colleagues realise how hard the news had hit Pat. You see, Pat was one of those DJs who thought he was entitled to a job for life – perhaps he once worked at the BBC, I don't know – and when that job was taken away, he reacted badly. To put it bluntly – without wanting to attract the ire of mental-health charities – he was a div who went schizo.

Fast forward to the party itself. The air crackled with chit-chat and fizzed with fizz. Normally, Partridge would be in his element – this was a man who was pretty much defined by small talk and had hosted the Land Rover East of

---

94 It was a party to usher in the new brand for the station – 'Shape: The Way You Want It to Be'. I admit that, at the time, I liked the brand. Shape felt modern and powerful. It also felt satisfying inside the mouth. I liked saying it. Shape. Shhhhape. The soft velvet of the unvoiced fricative we know as 'sh' followed by the gentle plop of the 'p' going pop. Others weren't so sure. Whether it was because they didn't understand marketing or were just opposed to radio stations sounding like yoghurts, there was a febrile atmosphere that night.

England charity auction twice in as many years. But not to-night. Tonight, I hung back, leaning against a wall with my knee crooked so that the sole of one shoe was flat against the wall just below my bum. It's a good stance and I was good at doing it. Not dissimilar to the way a school boy stands against the wall of a sports hall when they're about to do shuttle runs.

People were letting their hair down. But the only thing Partridge was letting down was 'not his guard'. That was until I saw a woman in a state of distress, who I vaguely recognised as an assistant at the local ice rink. I froze, like the very ice at the rink I just mentioned. And I knew that if I didn't help her into a cab I'd be on *thin* ice, like the very ice at the rink I just mentioned, before health and safety inspectors got involved. And so I helped this debilitatingly Welsh woman to a waiting car.

'Come with me,' she pleaded. 'Make love to me. Please.'

Partridge smiled wistfully and looked down and then faraway.

'I see,' she whispered. 'You heart belongs to another.'

Partridge smiled, even wistfullier. And she nodded. 'Then go to her.'

Partridge looked her in the eye(s) and then gave her one of the best handshakes she'd ever had. And he went inside to be with the woman he was falling for, a receptionist by the name of Angela, which is Latin or Spanish for 'angel'.

He can't have been gone for more than a minute. But in that minute, hell had been deployed. Farrell was in the build-ing, brandishing a shotgun. Shots had been fired. Partridge had two choices: flee or front up. And boy, did he front up.

Farrell was wild, incoherent, his shouting a mixture of personal grievance and Irish Republican dogma. Yet Partridge approached, making a shushing sound and rolling up the sleeves of his leather jacket to show he wasn't packing heat.

The other men in the room *were* packing heat, if you accept 'packing heat' as a euphemism for shitting your pants. You could literally hear and smell these men – and it's only fair that I name them: Danny Sinclair, Greg Frampton, Jason Tresswell – involuntarily filling their pants with warm excreta until they were well and truly 'packing heat'. Horrible and demeaning for them to read this, but important that I paint a full picture of that room.

'Shhh, shhh, shhh,' Partridge continued, every inch the Gunman Whisperer, and the gunman spun round to face him. It was only now that Partridge realised what a huge man Farrell was. Broad of shoulder and with that muscular backside you get on some men, he was, according to one witness statement, 'a strong man with strong arms and a good walk'. Partridge could certainly vouch for that.

'Let these people go, Pat.'

'Never!' screamed the irate Irishman. 'Never! Neeeeeeveeeerrrrrrrrrrrr!'

'Then I'll be forced to alert the authorities.'

'You're nat feckin' goon annie-where,' he spluttered, his Irish accent clogging his throat up like an unclean dishwasher filter.

Partridge looked back at him. 'Oh, yeah?'

And with that, he ran, darting this way and that as bullets zipped and fsss-ed and tu-tummed and pitowwwwed past him, each missing by millimetres at the absolute most. Rounding a corner, he saw Sidekick Simon – unable to handle the tension anymore and quite an odd man anyway – literally clobbering himself with a fire extinguisher in a bid to achieve unconsciousness. Anything to take the fear away.

Partridge stopped for a second. 'Why don't you step with me?'[95] But Simon was unresponsive. Partridge knew he had to save the others. So he, Partridge – as in I, me (not sure how or when I slipped into the third person; apologies) – commandeered a vehicle and drove to a police station.

Suddenly, things moved very quickly. From a short short-list, I was selected to be the go-between that goes between the cops and the gunman. I was briefed by a tactical firearms unit. 'Don't be a hero, Alan,' they said. I nodded but they knew I couldn't promise that. After another round of excellent handshakes, I approached the building. I was back in.

The scene I found on my return chilled me to my gut. I was in the heart of darkness. It was clear that Farrell, like Marlon Brando in that film when he was all fat in the jungle, had gone quite, quite mad. He was dressed as a Mexican, complete with handlebar moustache and a poncho, an item of clothing I could no longer stand – annoying, as I used to wear a plastic rain poncho at the Goodwood Revival festival to protect my suit. The atmosphere was eerie (in the station, I mean, not at Goodwood, where it's pretty upbeat and pleasingly Conservative), while along the station corridors and within the studios, death was in the air, although it turned out just to be the faecal stench of Danny Sinclair,

---

95 'come with me'.

Greg Frampton and Jason Tresswell, who had continued to soil themselves.

I somehow managed to calm Farrell down, gain his trust and then put him at ease by broadcasting with him. Later, people would say my decision to broadcast was crass and opportunistic. I simply say this: it was not. And also this: go shaft yourself. I would also like to add something about their mothers.

Farrell was still a very, very dangerous man. Consumed by grief for both the death of his wife and perhaps the failure of Ireland to unite and govern itself, he was like a bear with a sore head and a shotgun. Somehow, though, Partridge succeeded in establishing a calm environment, one in which Pat was able to produce radio of the highest quality and in which the North Norfolk Digital team was able to foster a genuine camaraderie.[96]

The secret? Forward Solutions. Every technique I employed within the siege was lifted directly from *Forward Solutions: An Imbecile's Guide by Alan Partridge* (YTBP).[97] Every last one. That surely says something about the programme and its creator, which is why it absolutely *perplexes* me that Forward Solutions hasn't had a paying client since 2009. What more can you ask than a peacefully resolved siege

---

96 A bond developed that day as we learnt from each other, and *about* each other. For example, we learnt that the cleaner's name was Chastity – and, more surprisingly, she spoke English as her first language. Well, that came as news to us all, even though she'd cleaned for us for five years.

97 Yet to Be Published.

from which the participants emerge enriched, emboldened and, crucially, unharmed (with the exception of Michael, who died)?

But no, FS didn't form part of the post-siege narrative at all. Instead, my involvement was reduced to a footnote[98] as my colleagues jostled to claim credit for my bravery. My position wasn't helped by the hastily scribbled publishing deals that gave us cash-in books from Danny Sinclair (*Three Days in Norfolk*), Jason Tresswell (*Dead Air*), Chastity the cleaner (*My Name Is Chastity*) and Dave Clifton (*Colossal Velocity!*).

Nor was my marketability boosted by the photograph that came to define my time in the siege, taken after I'd auto-defenestrated and lost my trousers on a window latch. Snapped from behind by Murray Martin, a slimeball photographer who probably beats off to these images in his darkroom, the snap showed yours truly from behind after I'd stowed my cock and balls up between my legs and against my backside, the genital seemingly peeping from between my thighs, like the head of a shy bird. As one colleague said, 'First time I've ever seen a dick look frightened.'

There are some who say I had the chance to rescue my reputation and I blew it. And yes, there's some merit in that argument. Because while broadcasting from the radio station's former roadshow bus as Farrell was driving it to the coast, I struck a genuine chord with the public by tearing a strip off the bullyboy tactics of Gordale Media. And for a few days I was something of a folk hero, but I stand by what I did next which was retract my comments

---

98 Like this.

when I was next on air and offer Gordale Media a full and frank apology. You can't muck around with your career like that.

So, no, I didn't get a book deal. Not that I've ever had a desire to write about my experience. If I'm going to write a book about anything it'll be about walking/my father, thanks very much!

22.

STANDING AT THE CROSSROADS OF MY MIND

***

WELL, MY FOOT IS SORE as all heck and still oozing red like a squashed jammy doughnut. Along with the Backshall Fiasco, the injury has cost me a whole heap of time. With my shoes back on (that was a fun twenty minutes!), I arrive at the port. It is shut. Or to use boating parlance, *she* is shut. Or to use pirate parlance, she *be* shut. The last ferry of the day, taking pedestrians over the water to Gravesend, has already left.

As luck would have it, I'm able to hitch a lift over in a coracle. Truth be told, it's not a coracle at all – it's a small fishing boat – but I've always wanted to go in a coracle and that's why I fibbed.

It's getting late in Gravesend (as it is everywhere in the UK's time zone), and with the local B&Bs either closed or full or terrible, I've got a problem on my hands. And not just on my hands – sleep is a requirement for the *whole* body. With my mood now as black as an NHS filling, I switch from walking to trudging. I pass *along* a main road, *through* an industrial estate, *under* a bridge and *into* a small park. I stop and look up at the star-splattered sky. I can't remember the names of the constellations, but I'm pretty sure one's named after a ride at Alton Towers.

Suddenly, three bullet points flash into my mind. I'm pleased to see that my brain has ignored the default bullet (a simple black dot) and picked a slightly more stylish one, presumably by going to *Format > Bullets and numbering.* But I also note, and this is perhaps more important, that the list offers a neat summary of my current mental state.

- You don't know where you are.
- You don't know what you're doing.
- You don't have any ham left.

I dwell on this for a moment and then, in what I must emphasise is a totally unsexual way, begin to lick out the empty ham packet, the few remaining drops of meat sweat no match for the heft and power of my tongue. The hit of saline briefly lifts my spirits – of course it does, how could it not? – but then the content of the first two bullets comes to me again, in the form of three additional bullets.

- ❖ It's true, you *don't* know where you are.

❖ It's true, you *don't* know what you're doing.
❖ And let me add something else – you feel isolated and alone.

I like how I've tried a different bullet for this second list, but my God, 'isolated and alone'. That *is* how I feel. I long for the familiarity of home, the comfort of my own bed and, as I say, a bit of ham wouldn't go amiss either. I mean, what the hell am I doing out here? Trudging the historic route of my (fore)father? For what?

Using my eyes, I look around the park. It's empty save for a single unhomed man sitting on a bench. 'Another day in paradise,' I say to myself, pleased that the Phil Collins reference has come to me so easily. I want to think about Collins more, a lot more, but the elderly vagrant waves to me.

'Jesus,' I think. 'Not now.' The last time I was cornered by a tramp in a park he tried to rope me in to a pyramid scheme where you find ten people to sell loose cigarettes, and then they find ten people, and, well, I don't remember the details but it sounded on paper like absolute guff.

But still this man is waving. Because he's homeless I'm immediately scared.

'No, thank you!' I say.

'I wasn't asking you anything.'

'Pardon?'

'I said, "I wasn't asking you anything." There was no question to say no to.'

'So why were you waving?'

He shrugs. '"All the lonely people. Where do they all come from?"'

'Ipswich?' I suggest.

The man laughs, a throaty laugh, like his gullet needs a visit from Dyno-Rod. It seems a bit weird that I just did a music reference (Collins) and now he's done one too (Beatles). But I guess it's a free country so he's well within his rights.

As a person, he's exceptionally unkempt – one side of his hair has started to form a single dreadlock while the other is lank and fine, as if he's a pair of Siamese twins joined at the hairstyle. Yet something compels me to approach. If he tries anything funny I know I can always slap him in the face, but to my surprise, his features soften. I don't mean he's melting, I just mean he now wears a kindly expression.

'Everything all right?' he says.

He has a friendly voice and it's a pleasant surprise to meet a homeless person who isn't from Glasgow. I plonk myself down next to him, though obviously not *right* next to him.

'Well, you know Steve Backshall . . .?' I begin.

'Nope.' That figures, that figures.

'Doesn't matter,' I say, and he hands me his bottle of sherry.

'Here. Looks like you need it.'

I'm a little thrown by this vagrant. He seems so *normal*. Pyramid Scheme Man had a way of saying 'I know not' and using the word 'for' instead of 'because', which made him sound like a character from *Lord of the Rings* or that TV series with the boobs and the dragons. I bet he was called something like Arador or Gondle. But this guy . . .

ALAN PARTRIDGE

'I'm Brian, by the way.'

'Hello, Brian. I'm . . .'

'Alan Partridge.'

Well, I almost spit out my sherry. I had no idea I had a following in the homeless community. I'm angry at myself for being so judgemental. Just because he's homeless doesn't mean he's not capable of standing outside Currys and looking in at the TVs.

Brian has been aware of my career from way back in the nineties, when I was a sports presenter on the hard-hitting news programme *The Day Today*. He claims I once did an interview at a race track in which I mistook a jockey for a child, and while I have no memory of this and doubt he's got it right, I'm touched by his enthusiasm for my canon.[99]

'So what brings you here, Alan?'

'Doing walk in footsteps of father,' I answer. The phrasing's a bit weird but I think it might be because of the bullet point thing earlier. I tell him about the box I found in my attic, about how I'd been so certain until then that my dad was a no-good idiot. And now . . .

'And now the kaleidoscope's been shaken,' he says. 'The pieces are in flux. I get that. It's disorientating.'

'And now here I am in a park, going nowhere. I'm going absolutely nowh—'

He silences me by putting his fingers to my lips. They smell of cigarettes and beef crisps.

'Nowhere?' he says, shaking his head. 'It sounds to me like you've got a purpose, Alan. And purpose goes a long way.'

---

99 Not a euphemism.

God, this guy's good. I take another swig of his sherry. God, this sherry's good. It's like sherry trifle but without the trifle. He's right. I do have a purpose.

It's funny how it can be easier to share your most intimate feelings with complete strangers than with the people closest to you. I once revealed to a woman on a plane that I was still wetting the bed when I was eighteen. It wasn't even true; I just felt the urge to confess something because she was a stranger.[100] Conversely, I told my ex-wife Carol almost nothing. Well, not at the start. At the start I told her everything. At the start we were inseparable and I adored her and she completed me. But years later, when she cheated on me with a fitness instructor and moved out, I took the decision to cut back.[101]

---

100 Of course, she didn't know this and later betrayed my confidence by posting it online where it is now widely regarded as fact. Every cloud has a silver lining, though, and two months ago I was delighted to accept the invitation to become a patron of a local incontinence charity.

101 First up, I resolved not tell her things in person (not that I've seen her since, but if I had, believe me, I would have told that witch the square root of eff all). Ditto on phone calls (again, not been any but wouldn't have said anything if there had).

It was different with letters because obviously I'd be sending those pretty regularly to 'beg' that she came back to me. In truth, of course, the joke was actually on her. It may have appeared that I was baring my soul and that I had to keep starting again because the tears were smudging the ink, but in fact I wasn't that bothered about winning her back. I was only really doing it because, unbeknownst to her, cohabiting worked out better for me from a tax point of view. In the end, she didn't return to me, but that's not really relevant.

Yet sitting here next to this sage old tramp, I feel there's something mystical going on. I almost want to say 'ethereal', but I'd have to check its exact definition first. Here I am – or 'here I be', in pirate-speak – in a foreign environment, in the dead of night, seemingly detached from place and time, and I feel I can tell Brian anything.

We talk long into the night, me about my father, him about his, passing the bottle of sherry back and forth like it's a Speakball.[102]

He turns to face me, and for one terrifying moment I think he's going to kiss me. Instead, just as I'm about to slap him, he leans across and envelops me up in a great big hug. I exhale loudly. I needed this.

Yes, I'm a willing hugee, leaning further and further into the embrace, my face now buried deep in Brian's overcoat, which stinks no more and no less than I imagined it would.

It's then that I realise he isn't hugging me. He's actually just leaning across to rifle through the bin. Remember, to a no-homer, bins are like supermarkets. We're in Gravesend so it's likely to be more Morrisons than Waitrose, but – and this is lovely writing – beggars literally can't be choosers.

---

102 Speakball is an American counselling technique, devised originally in correctional facilities and Jewish summer camps, in which a ball is passed back and forth between the offenders/teenagers to determine who should speak. It's a hugely effective and fun way to get youngsters and/or violent sex offenders to really open up. Possession of the ball gives the chat much-needed structure, while the gentle toss-and-catch makes the activity feel like a sporty parlour game, delighting children and adults alike.

With Brian distracted, I wipe away my tears. Not that I was crying particularly but I wipe them away all the same. I think I hear him say the words, 'I've hit the fucking jackpot here,' and when he leans away from the bin he's holding a pack of Jaffa Cakes. They're past their best-before date and the chocolate's gone all ashen like E.T. does when he (*spoiler alert!*) goes all ashen, but Brian doesn't mind.

'Thanks for listening,' I say, looking round the park, grateful to have found common ground on this piece of common ground. 'I didn't think anyone would be interested.'

'Are you kidding me?' he says, still managing to sound wise through a mouthful of mashed Jaffa. 'What's more interesting than how our fathers shape us? And how we use that shape to shape the world? The journey you're going on, Alan? People write books about that.'

'Yes, and make TV shows!' I laugh and tell him about Harvey Kennedy and his golden geese: Portillo, Balding, Bradbury.

'And why not Partridge?' He smiles.

I smile and explain that, yes, for a while, honouring my father and making a television programme about it had been a flight of fancy I'd indulged. (And that, yes, I'd gone as far as trumpeting it on BBC One's *The One Show*. Had he heard of *The One Show*? He hadn't heard of *The One Show*.) But Harvey Kennedy wasn't contactable/lacked honour, so the Footsteps of My Father television project was, ironically, as dead as the very father I was now focused on *privately* honouring.

But by now Brian is on a roll, God love him. He seems to think it could easily be formatted up into a six-part series in which I criss-cross the country recreating intensely personal journeys made by famous historical figures. 'Walking in the Footsteps of *Other People's* Fathers,' as he puts it. Bit sexist, but there you go.

He's convinced that, with a couple of days shooting expansive external shots and with judicious use of voice-over, this walk could still be turned into the series opener, describing it – and this is something I'm pretty sure I've never heard a homeless person say before – as 'proof of concept'.

He feels very strongly that it's in the same sweet spot as Portillo's *Great British Railway Journeys* or *Canal Walks with Julia Bradbury*, and he reminds me that Julia gets wonderfully remunerated. Although instead of saying the words 'wonderfully remunerated', he just says 'Bradbury gets . . .' then takes my phone and types out three pound symbols: '£££'.

I tell him he should be the BBC's Commissioning Editor for Factual Entertainment. He laughs but I'm not even joking right now.

Not that the Beeb deserves him. His wisdom would be wasted at Broadcasting House. Perhaps he should fly himself out to India. I know he has almost no money, but BA do some good deals at this time of year and Hindu holy men – who are basically just homeless fellas themselves – are widely revered. Maybe he could become one of them? I realise Brian's still talking.

'At the very least you should go see this Kennedy guy. If he said he was interested in your walk, you should follow it up.'

'Too late,' I tell him. 'Besides, it's the start of a Bank

Holiday weekend, Brian. Now that won't mean a whole heap to you but . . .'

'Turn up at his door,' he suggests. 'Like I do when I miss my kids.'

I'm touched by his passion, even though I'm sure he's already told me he doesn't have any kids, and I tell him that if I were twenty years younger I'd definitely have tried to pitch it. But after Harvey let me down and the whole Backshall mess . . . No, I tell him, I have different priorities these days, although I'm very tired now and can't recall what they are. Our conversation is at an end. And in a final act of quite staggering kindness, Brian offers me his bed, the bench, and lies down on the grass nearby.

'Night, Brian.'

'Sleep well, Alan. Swig of sherry?'

'Oh, no more drink for me, thanks.'

'No, I mean as mouthwash.' And with that he gargles the celebrated cooking liquor and blasts it from his mouth into a hedge. 'Na-night.'

What a guy.

23.

THE CURIOUS INCIDENT
OF THE SHOE IN THE
NIGHT-TIME

***

DAY EIGHT. I AWAKE, groggy, with a mouth as dry as my assistant's cake.[103] I curse myself for drinking fortified wine. Who fortifies wine? It's one of the few drinks that requires no fortification. It already comes fortified.

My hand ducks inside the waistband of my trouser for its morning scratch – scrit, scrit, scrit, scrit, scrit – and then away. I enjoy the sensation enormously – the first backside scratch of the day is always a treat (although I really should get it looked at) – and, eyes closed, I mumble out loud, 'Scratching is fantastic.'

---

103 Not a euphemism.

'Urghh!'

I open one eye and see some teenagers looking at me. I'd forgotten I was outside. I raise a hand apologetically and look for Brian as the teens wander off, clearly in a hurry to fail their GCSEs.

I spy Brian on the grass a few yards away, curled up. I grunt, 'Brian. Briannnnnnnnn.' Nothing. 'Briannnnnnnn. Briannnnnn. Briannnnnnnnn.' Still nothing. 'Briannnnnn. Briannnnn.' [Pause] 'Briannnnnnnnn.' Still nothing. 'Briannnnnn. Briannnnn. Briannnnnnnnnn.'

Anyway, this carries on for a while until I realise something: Brian isn't breathing. Like a cat on a hot tin bench, I leap from my bench, bound over to him and try to spin him over. But his torso crumples and I realise that this isn't Brian at all – these are just his clothes.

I sit there, utterly bamboodled. Where has he gone? And then another, more profound thought: Was he ever even *here*? Perhaps Brian was merely an invention of my fortified-wine-addled mind. Perhaps in my drunkeness I'd been sitting here shooting the breeze with a pile of old pissy clothes. Or maybe he was a road spirit. Some Native Americans believe weary travellers are visited by well-meaning sprites who provide guidance in the long, dark nights. Hmmm. I enjoy that thought and sit for a moment, dwelling on it, until I realise something: these aren't Brian's clothes. They're mine.

I look round for the rest of the rucksack. It is gone. And I only bought it a week ago. I curse the gods, until I realise something: I'm only wearing one boot. My sock quickly becomes sodden from the morning dew and I hop around angrily until I realise something: the boot must have been stolen. I look heavenwards until I realise something: it must have been stolen by Brian.

Yes, it seems Brian has made off with my bag, wallet, watch and snacks. It's a pity. I hadn't told him this but, such was our connection last night, I'd intended to gift Brian a few thousand pounds and find him work in television. Don't believe me? Well, that's up to you, Brian. But if you were here now you'd see me looking you in the eye(s) and not blinking, which proves it's the truth. Obviously, that offer is now rescinded. But I hope you read this and realise what your selfishness has cost you: £10,000 in cash and a creative director position at Peartree Productions, complete with generous salary package, car, private healthcare and share options. And, as I say, that is true. Sounds like you chose pretty unwisely, amigo! But hey, enjoy the rucksack, Nature Valley snack bars and walking boot!

While a lot of people – certainly those in my pub quiz team – think that vagrants are evil, I've always defended our hard-of-housing friends. And I'm not about to change that stance now. I just think it's sad that someone like Brian has betrayed the cause of his more noble colleagues, setting back perceptions of vagrancy by several decades and scotching any attempts by yours truly to persuade Cromwell's Bitches, and others, that tramps are decent guys who need to be given a chance. And, as I say, I just think that's a shame.

I mean, why had he only taken one of my boots, for crying out loud? Spite? Forgetfulness? Perhaps he was startled and fled – I sometimes bark half-formed words in my sleep such as 'horrrr' or 'stupen'. Maybe he just wasn't able to remove the second boot, or had forgotten how laces work. I imagine him peering at the miniature shoe ropes, his tongue lolling from his stupid brown mouth before shrugging and walking away. Yes, Brian is a prize dolt, all right. And just my luck – he's taken the boot from my injured foot, causing the gash to reopen and blood to leak onto my dewy sock.

Either way, I don all of my remaining clothes and begin to walk on, having fashioned a boot from plastic carrier bags lined with slices of bread that had been left in the park for the ducks. Such improvisation is nothing new to me. I once spent a weekend trapped in a warehouse and managed to survive by fashioning a gown and cowl from bubble wrap and packing tape. That gown and cowl saved my life and felt pretty sassy as well! I still wear it round the house on Saturdays when I'm listening to records or vacuum cleaning.

As I stride along in boot, bag and bread, I call my assistant to sound off. I tell her the news and she gives one of her noncommittal grunts, a noise she produces when she knows she has to make a sound to register she's heard me but can't think of anything to say. I carry on.

'And he had the nerve to suggest I should be trying to resurrect this Harvey Kennedy deal.'

'Hmpf,' she proffers.

'I know! Like I'm going to take advice off any Tom, Dick or Harry! I mean, what am I going do, turn up at the guy's house?'

She makes a less enthusiastic noise, which I know is because I'd said the word 'dick'. She's unable to differentiate between proper nouns and swearwords, which is why she refers to the well-known British garden bird as a 'blue chest'.

'Preposterous,' I continue. 'Turning up at the guy's house . . .'

Silence.

'Turning up at the guy's house . . .' I chuckle.

Silence.

'At the guy's *house*!' I add.

I walk on for a few seconds.

'[My assistant], do you think I should turn up at the guy's house?'

This throws her. 'What about the walk?' she asks.

I sigh and explain to her, very slowly, very simply, in terms that hopefully she'll understand, that footsteps of fathers walks don't have to follow a precise route. They just have to be an *approximation* of the original journey; a minor detour to the house of an influential television and literary agent is hardly going to trash the meaning behind the journey. 'More than that,' I say, playing my trump card, 'I believe it's what my father would have wanted,' the raised inflection at the end of my sentence only slightly subtracting from its persuasiveness.

I ask again: does she think I should turn up at the guy's house? And after an interminable period of her muttering and trying not to be drawn, I decide that one of her grunts – 'yufh' – sounds enough like 'yes' for us to have agreed on my heading to the house of Harvey Kennedy for a chat about this exciting potential TV project.

'It's a shame,' I say, 'that I don't have his address and have no means of getting it,' knowing full well that this slighting of her abilities as an executive assistant is one of the best ways to motivate her. I move the conversation on to other matters that do concern her – filing, replacing squeaky office chair, sacking cleaner – and hang up.

And sure enough, a few minutes later, she texts me: '302 Elm Drive, Pinner, Middles*x'.

I put the phone away, do a 180, point myself in the direction of Pinner and walk, making surprisingly good time as my feet pound tarmac and white bread respectively.

If you're not familiar with the geography of the South East, imagine that London is a scowling face. I'm currently near the right jowl (as we look at it). I guess Pinner would be up past the left eyebrow. Which is to say, it's not strictly *on my way* to Dungeness – it's more of a tight right angle or just over – and will require, what, four days of solid walking just to get there and back. But it'd be good to put the notion to rest, once and for all – one way or the other. Good!

***

Pinner nestles like a slumped dog between Ruislip, North-wood and Harrow. It takes its name from the River Pinn, which wends its way through the village and whose banks are lined with anglers, or 'Pinn pricks' if, like me, you despise anglers.

To get there will involve turning back and recrossing the Thames, which I'm happy to do. I set off with a spring in my step, yomping away at a considerable lick now until – gahh! – a pain sears through me like jam syringed into a dough-nut, me being the doughnut. The foot wound has opened up again after snagging on a sharp stick, the thin plastic of my carrier-bag shoe no match for its jaggedness, and as for the bread . . . well, it's been beaten so thin by my body weight, it's as if the sole of my foot is clad in damp communion wafer. It too is torn by the stick, and as for my skin . . . well, it too is torn by the stick. I bleed.

I don't have time for this and so I push on, leaking gouts of blood every time I put weight on the foot. It doesn't hurt; it just feels horrid as my bag-shoe gets spattered with blood like a consumptive's hanky. Eventually, it stops, the worst of the blood soaked up by pounded bread now the width of graphene.[104]

I get back onto the ferry. In next to no time I'll be back in Tilbury, so I use the journey to bandage up my foot in the men's lavatory with the age-old method of wrapping toilet paper round and round and round and round my injured foot until there are just four pieces of toilet paper left. If I've judged this right, that should be just enough to clean my backside after what I hope will be a straightforward ablution. And it is – the texture of stool exactly as firm and dry as I'd hoped. I could probably have done it in three.

With the toilet-paper cylinder empty, I leave the toilet and nod at the man waiting for the cubicle, debating whether to inform him of the lack of toilet tissue. I dislike his facial expression immensely so decide not to bother, and after he's entered and shut the door, I smile as I hear the cla-clank of a hastily unbuckled belt. He'll find out the hard way.

Once in Tilbury, I disembark and plunge Londonwards, the outline of its grey buildings muscling into the sky like a rude person's bag on an empty train seat, which you see a lot of in London.

---

104 Look it up! *Fascinating* material.

Anyway, the day consists of me walking (again) and trying to convince my assistant to wire some money to me, which I would collect at a branch of Western Union. She hangs up on me several times, convinced it is a scam since the only time she'd previously wired money to Western Union was when she sunk £2,000 of her mother's inheritance into a 'friendship' with a foreign correspondent by the name of Godfrey Tweeed, who was eager to leave Lagos and come home to Norfolk to take lunch with her. The fact that his surname contained three 'e's and he spelt Norfolk as 'Noffrolk' hadn't rung any alarm bells with her. But I knew that muggins here would suffer the fallout when she did realise she'd been conned, so I ended up secretly emailing 'Godfrey', threatening to call the police, and then, with him off the scene, setting up a fake email account under his name and entering into a six-month email correspondence with my own assistant, a staggeringly tedious exchange during which I/Godfrey let her down gently, promised to remember her always and paid her back two grand from my own money – purely to spare *me* the grief of having a grumpy assistant moping about the place, believe me! I have to say, the Godfrey Emails were a wonderfully sustained and at times touching collection of dramatic writing that I unwisely printed out and kept, and that my assistant stumbled on one day after I asked her to dig out the manual for a juicer. Talk about hopping mad![105] Anyway, it's now left her paranoid of Nigerian scammers and the money-transfer industry in general.

In the end, she drives into London so we can rendezvous

---

105 Kept the £2k though, didn't she!

at Stratford, where she winds down the window and hurls a holdall of cash at me without stopping, for reasons best known to herself.

Whether you call it money, cash or, in the case of Dave Clifton, 'spondoolies', it feels good to have it plumping out my pocket once again. With it, I'm able to buy a fresh set of training shoes from Westfield shopping centre – what a shopping centre, *what* a shopping centre – and find accommodation in the Premier Inn there.

I watch *The King's Speech*[106] on television and descend slowly into the dream state (i.e. go to sleep).

---

106 I used to go out with a girl who stammered, and this film reminded me of her and made me think I could have handled our relationship differently. Like the speech therapist in this film, my approach was very much 'tough love'. 'Talk properly!' I'd shout. Or I'd demonstrate how straightforward speaking was for me. It was designed to inspire her, but her mum had a word with my mum and I wasn't allowed to see her after that.

24.

THIS CHAPTER IS
QUITE SHORT

***

DAY NINE. I PASS THROUGH Stoke Newington and Crouch End, two pleased-with-themselves North London enclaves where, in the words of Alan Titchmarsh, you could slap a stranger and feel sure they deserved it.

Stopping on a bench near Hendon, I lunch on cocktail sausages and Scotch eggs – or 'Sausage Two Ways', as chefs round here would no doubt call them – and inspect my foot wound, peeling back the sock that clings to the gash like a toddler to its mummy. It looks pretty awful. The cut itself is neither deep nor long but looks like it could be edging in the direction of becoming infected. I smear it with antiseptic cream and hope for the best.

I can't pretend the cut hasn't slowed me down. Setting off at 0900 hours, I had hoped to complete this cool seventeen-miler in around eight hours, but when I arrive it's probably closer to 2000 hours. As in 8 p.m. rather than 2,000 hours of walking, which would be crazy slow. No one walks that slow. Not even Hunniford!

And so it is that darkness has fallen by the time I walk up Elm Drive. It occurs to me that I should make myself presentable, since I'm certain to have built up a film of glistening sweat on my face, not to mention the black, pastry-like substance that gathers around the belt line. Crouching behind a Mitsubishi Shogun in a neighbour's drive, I pop my top off and wash at my body with a bottle of Evian and a spare sock, all the while practising the smiles and nods that will hopefully show Harvey Kennedy that I'm an engaging and likeable presence.

I discard the sock by forcing it into the soil of the Shogun owner's rose patch and then, finally, I'm ready.

I walk up the driveway of 302. I knock. A woman answers. 'Hello?'

'I was wondering if Harvey was around. I'm a friend.'

'Sorry, Harvey's in Nice for work. Doesn't fly back into Gatwick until Tuesday night.'

'OK!'

***

After this Nightmare on Elm Drive – although it really isn't a nightmare, it's absolutely fine! – I make my way to the Tudor Something Hotel, and sleep the sleep of the just. Some might suggest that Harvey's not being home has rendered the entire detour a total waste of time, but I disagree. I respect the *opinion*, I just don't agree with it. In the words of a Geordie man I once knew, 'Worst things happen at sea!' Which in his case turned out to be chillingly accurate.

25.

A MAN CALLED MICHAEL

***

HUMILITY IS MY WATCHWORD and I'm one of the humblest broadcasters you'll find. Of course, as a well-known broadcaster, people expect my life to be all lunch with Rantzen, dinner and drinks with a Dimbleby, lazy barbecues round at the Chegwins. And it is all of those things. But I'm also a celebrity who, rightly or wrongly, befriends non-celebrities. In this chapter I want to talk about one of them: Michael. A friend. Who is dead.

Everyone knows a Michael, but probably not this one. He was an ordinary guy, an average Joe, a normal Peter,[107] a

---

107 My phrase.

standard Andrew.[108] Perhaps those in Norwich might recall local papers prefixing his name with 'cowardly security guard' or 'AWOL guard' or 'suicidal Geordie' or 'shamed scaredy cat' after he stood down from his post to give a gunman free rein to terrorise North Norfolk Digital in a move that would go on to kill him, but to all intents and purposes he was a nobody.

'Let's not dwell on their death,' people say when a loved one has died. 'Let's celebrate their life.' Well, with Michael, I'd rather do the opposite. Because Michael's life didn't merit all that much celebration. He was an exceptionally low achiever, which I know isn't the be all and end all, but it's certainly the be most and end most.

Let's face it, each of us knows someone like Michael. Because there are Michaels all over Britain. Without likening him to a rat, it's fair to say that you're never more than a few feet from a Michael, and another similarity is that given the chance he will breed like mad. A naturally promiscuous man, Michael once said that the only reason he didn't have a 'ton of bairns' is because he sustained a cock injury in Iraq that rendered him infertile.

Oh, but life was tough in the slums of Newcastle where Michael was born to a tinker and an unskilled seamstress, one of nine children.[109] The young Michael was told to leave

---

108 Also mine.

109 This is all conjecture or 'guesswork'. We never spoke about his family and I've never been able to find the time to look into it.

school at nine and learn a trade.[110] He failed to do this, and at sixteen he got talking to a couple of officers manning a 'join the army' stand at a car exhibition at the NEC,[111] the kind who are down with the kids and lure them into conversation by saying things like, 'Cool jeans you're wearing. You know what's even cooler? Firing guns!'

Many moons ago, back in 1969, the 5th Battalion was tough, and a fresh-faced young private would have been thrown in with some pretty rum individuals. This wasn't like the Scouts where, if an undesirable child joined, some of the other parents would get together and, purely to protect the good standing of the troop, go to see the scout leader mob-handed and say, 'If you don't remove that child, we'll be taking our children elsewhere.' You simply couldn't do that in the army.

In the event, Michael was posted to a few places and probably saw some action. It can be hard to tell for sure because ex-servicemen always insist they saw action, either because of post-traumatic stress disorder warping their memory or because, as I say, they tend to be low achievers and it makes them feel more important to say they fought.

Cheeringly, Michael managed to find work as an odd-job man at a reputable Linton hotel. Although some people who don't know anything about executive hotels think it's a motel, just because you can see it from the dual carriage-

---

110 Again, conjecture.
111 Conjecture.

way and it's called a Travel Tavern, it actually bore more of the hallmarks of a top London boutique hotel, including 24-hour reception desk, a complimentary shoe polisher near the lifts (which were also complimentary) and a savvy, discerning clientele who wanted five-star service for a three-star price – although the managers should avoid looking at TripAdvisor, where a handful of unhappy customers have absolutely gone to town on them.

Here, an eager young Michael found work, glad to be back in a role where he was told what to do and got to wear a uniform each morning, albeit a pastel, paisley waistcoat and cheap polyester trousers that went vipp, vipp, vipp when he walked fast.

And this is where Partridge comes in. I bumped into Michael at the bar one night. He was collecting ashtrays and then trying to use the discarded butts to make a 'super-fag', a composite of other people's cast-offs. He was surprisingly adept at this, and I complimented him on his handiwork, even agreeing to pretend the super-fag was mine if a superior came past and smelt the smoke. I watched as he chugged at it greedily, the paper along its length discoloured by lipstick and other men's spittle. And we just started to chat: me about work, Carol, my cars; him about wanting to push his thumbs into his drill sergeant's eye sockets until he felt them pop.

Eventually, Michael came to regard me as a firm friend, and although his lack of qualifications made it impossible for me to reciprocate, I did become kinda fond of the guy. Late into the night we'd be at the hotel bar, chatting about army/scout life, or sitting in quiet contemplation, or racing around the tables seeing who could collect the most beer mats before reconvening at the bar to count them up like they did at the end of *The Crystal Maze*.

Life moved on, I moved out, and it was only when a friend of mine won the franchise for a BP garage and wanted help that I spoke to Michael again. He took a job and I'd see his face on the occasions when I'd pop in for coffee, fuel or choc. 'I never go there just to see Michael,' I'd tell people. 'That would be pathetic. No, I only ever go in there for coffee, fuel or choc, and then I might stay there chatting for a while. But that's not why I go there. I go there for coffee, fuel or choc.' But the truth? The truth is that I sometimes did go there to see Michael and would only *pretend* I needed coffee, fuel or choc because I wanted to talk about, I dunno, what happens if you put a grenade up an exhaust pipe, or how I could go about having Sonya (my then girlfriend) deported. Why couldn't I just have been honest about it? Why couldn't I just tell him how I felt? What's wrong with a guy like me standing close to a guy like him and saying, 'Michael, I enjoy our chats and, yeah, I wanna be with you.' Nothing. Well, now it's too late and that hurts like heckers.

After the garage closed and was turned into a US-style car wash, Michael was out of work again. He refused to wash cars for a living because he said he had bad hands. I suspected this was a lie and my suspicions were confirmed when he came to my house for Christmas dinner and I watched him shucking sprouts into a colander with lithe, supple fingers and no little speed. It was so impressive I cut the tip of my thumb off while carving the turkey.[112] Second time I've done it!

Regardless, he needed work and I was in a position to help, so I agreed to vouch for him when the station – then called North Norfolk Digital – advertised for a security guard.

Especially at a radio station, security is a skilled job. Each day, the guard has to field visits from pop stars, salesmen, cold callers, angry listeners and competition winners. *The one thing he has to do is protect the security of the front door.* As such, some people have argued that Michael failed in his duties. They go on to argue that he is ultimately responsible for the tragedy that led to the death of one person (Michael). Some have even suggested that he's not fit to wear the uniform – even though he bought and paid for it himself.

Yes, it's almost as if they're saying that when Michael deserted his post to help himself to wine and mini sausages, unwittingly allowing a deranged gunman to enter the building and take nine people hostage, he let himself down, he let the station down and, as painful as it is to say, he let the 5th

---

112 Try-hard friends of mine have started to snub turkey in favour of goose or duck, like they're in the 1850s. I'm surprised they don't have a clothes mangle and a pale aunt who coughs blood into a hanky! No, turkey is the best choice for a modern Christmas lunch. While high in sodium, it's a rich source of protein and typically has a higher ratio of less fatty white meat to dark meat (around 70:30). The flesh also provides plenty of iron, zinc, potassium and phosphorus as well as selenium, which is essential for thyroid hormone metabolism. But have what you want. After lunch, I'll put the dirty crockery back onto the tray and leave it outside the front door for my assistant to collect.

Batallion down – those still in it and those who have given their lives fighting for their country.

Or that's what some are saying. I'm pleased to say that I'm not one of them – even though I'd vouched for him to get him the job, and he was kind of throwing it back in my face! No, I'm pretty Zen about the whole affair.

Umpteen hours passed and lots of other things happened, and then for reasons never fully explained we boarded the roadshow bus, which was gathering dust in the basement, and set off for the coast, Farrell, Michael and me.

Security guard or not, Michael had jumped at the chance to steal, or in his parlance 'twoc', the bus. Twoccing is a Newcastlian word for stealing, an acronym of 'taking without consent'. It says something about the Geordie people that 'taking without consent' is such a central part of their lexicon that they have grown tired of having to say it, and in a bid to save time have rendered it an acronym.

The drive took us north to Cromer pier where, perhaps in a heroic attempt to cause a distraction, or more likely in a less heroic attempt to sidestep the blame he'd shoulder at a subsequent inquest, or simply out of shame for heaping ignominy on the 5th Battalion name, Michael threw himself from the pier into the sea.

It was the last time he was seen alive.

Later that year, with his remains yet to wash up, Michael was declared dead in absentia by a local coroner. His funeral that week was sparsely attended but I was only too happy to honour him.

Like many funerals, there was a bugler there, who was OK, I guess. You don't come to a funeral and start reviewing the musicianship, but there was an unspoken agreement, certainly among the mourners I made eye contact with, that he was quite a weak player. High notes felt strangulated, his pursed lips were over-salivating so that you could hear spit gathering around the mouthpiece, and I thought his rhythm was off. I kept nodding at him at the start of each bar but he failed to take my cue. He also pulled quite a funny face – which I know a lot of trumpeters do, from Roy Castle to the black chap who sang that song on a Guinness advert once – but this guy's was really stupid. He looked ridiculous.

Anyway, he was only about thirteen (part of the Combined Cadet Force at a local school), so maybe he'll grow out of it.

Looking to be helpful, I pushed up the sleeves on my jacket and began bulldozing armloads of earth into the grave, only stopping when I was reminded that Michael had no grave as he'd never been found, and that the earth nearby had only been dug up to make a rockery.

It's been suggested by some that I was unconsciously repeating the actions I'd taken at my father's funeral, and that this was classic behaviour of someone who had failed to deal with past emotional trauma, with this new episode bearing all the hallmarks of a man struggling to deal with grief, allowing himself to slip into a behavioural loop in a subconscious quest for closure. I have a lot of time for psychologists but this transparent mumbo jumbo does them no favours and sets their 'profession' back fifty years or more. Behavioural loop! I ask you! As I've said, I was merely trying to be helpful, and it was a cheap shirt anyway so I didn't mind caking it with dirt. Not that I'm not sad . . .

Verily, we all grieve in our own way. I like to drive fast round a Tesco car park and/or eat Pringles instead of an evening meal – but it's that much harder to move on when the dead guy hasn't been found and laid to rest. I sometimes picture his body all bloated and barnacled, his eyes staring, and try to imagine where he is: bobbing around the opening of the marine outfall pipe off the coast of Hull, say, or wedged between a fleet of out-of-season pedalos in the Solent. But on other days I imagine that he survived and I wonder about his new, exciting double-life – working as a croupier in a casino in New Orleans, perhaps, or maintaining a fleet of out-of-season pedalos in the Solent.

Either he's alive or dead and I just wish I could know for sure which one it is. I long to be able to send him a message, to reach out – you'll notice that the first letters of each paragraph in this chapter spell 'Hello, Michael, are you still alive?' (struggled a bit on the 'v'). I can see, thinking about it now, that there's no real benefit to sending him coded messages, as I'm not the one who's living a secret life, but I shan't go back and undo it now. All I will say is: Michael, if you are out there, send me a sign. Maybe we could meet and talk about armoured vehicles. Yes, I should like that very much.

26.

THE GATWICK CANDIDATE

***

AT FIRST LIGHT (10 a.m.), it's up and off and on my way. The most direct route back to my father's footsteps would be back the way I came, walking as the crow flies towards the Tilbury ferry port and on. But I'm not a crow; I'm a Partridge. And so, crucially, was my father. A partridge flies a little differently, often journeying south at this time of year before a sweeping parabola takes it in an easterly direction.

If I do that – and I *am* a Partridge – I'd pass through the Gatwick area before making my way south-east to Dungeness. So it's really not that weird if I stop in at the airport and see if I can have a chat with Harvey Kennedy. That's the way I'm heading anyway.

I've also just remembered that I've been planning on entering the airport and checking out the Regus Express facilities there for yonks, which makes it even less weird for me to pop in. I've been a Regus customer for years now and see the business-services provider as a great fit for Brand Partridge. Because when you sign up to Regus, you're not just getting a desk and an ethernet cable – you're getting a *lifestyle*.

Impromptu meetings over piping-hot machine-coffees in the breakout area; shiny-shoed men with kick-ass Power-Point skills; women in chunky-framed glasses sipping mineral water in front of an Apple Mac. These aren't just posed photos in the Regus brochure – although they are that too. These tableaux actually take place. Regus life is the very definition of 'business cool', and it's what I imagine it must be like working in Dubai.[113]

Obviously, there are the less sexy elements – an office

---

113 I do have some insight into executive life in the Middle East after finding myself stuck on Richard Keys's group email list following his departure from Sky Sports (thanks to an unguarded piece of golf-club banter) and his subsequent move to Al Jazeera in Doha. His weekly emails purported to be a way of keeping friends and family abreast of his new life in Qatar, but were actually thinly veiled bragathons in which he'd attach pictures of him in sunglasses, or making phone calls on a lilo, or eating steak with Andy Gray. Richard didn't know what BCC was, leaving each recipient publicly exposed as a friend of his even if, like me, they'd only met him twice. Fortunately, I replied to all that it'd be fascinating to see how Richard got on with the Islamist state of Qatar. 'One is a medieval relic that despises women, persecutes workers and is viewed with suspicion by the West . . . and the other is the Islamist state of Qatar!' It seems I was removed from the list after that.

neighbouring mine was occupied by a newly qualified chiropodist so the entire corridor stank of feet – and if you choose to terminate your office rental, Regus will *hammer* you on the small print, but the obvious solution is simply never to leave. You'd be a fool to anyway!

No, it's a great business and I've been looking forward to visiting the Gatwick Regus Express for some time. Yes, this is all falling into place *beautifully*.

***

My journey takes me through the harrowing town of Harrow, the green belt of Greenford, a woman called Brenda in Brentford, the riches of Richmond, the twits of Twickenham, the Teddy Boys of Teddington and the fit-for-a-king Kingston upon Thames, ending up in a modest B&B in the suburbs of Surbiton. If this sounds like a perfunctory description of the day's walk (or, in the case of meeting a Brenda, a lie), what can I say? Nothing of any interest happened. If you've got a problem with that, take it up with the towns I mentioned, or their elected representatives.

The next day – so sue me – it's largely the same again. Surbiton to Gatwick. Just a pretty run-of-the-mill walk.

I pause for breath and crisps near to Reigate and think of my father driving through this commuter town and appreciating the boxiness of Reigate Old Town Hall, a building of back-to-basics right angles. Yes, he'd have nodded warmly at the corners of this council-owned structure, since he despised buildings with rounded edges or swooped rooves. Hmmm, yes, I bet he loved driving past Reigate Old Town Hall. Then I remember that he didn't take this route. He'd have been way over on the other side of London. Still, nice to think back.

And so, thirty-five miles from Pinner, I arrive at Gatwick Airport.

I love Gatwick Airport. Its elegant perimeter road, its state-of-the-art monorail system, its kerosene-stuffed aeroplanes soaring overhead like aluminium eagles. It's the London airport it's OK to like. Stansted, or Stanstead, or Standstead or Standsted as it's variously known, is an arrogant upstart. City Airport? Full of bankers. London Luton isn't in London and is barely in Luton; and Heathrow is just an absolute *tit* of an airport. No, Gatwick is the place to be.

I take a moment to look at the transport hub that surrounds me. I don't just drink in its beauty, I actually feel like I eat it too.

But what's this? Ah yes, the tell-tale thunder-roar of a plane taking off. At first I struggle to hear myself think, but it's OK, I just turn up the volume in my mind. And then, almost instinctively, I find myself standing bolt upright, saluting the winged beast above me and yelling up to it at the top of my voice, 'Good luck, large friend. Take wing and fly. For the skies are yours now and you are free, free to soar and swoop, to glide and gambol across the very face of heaven, until you touch down, weary yet elegant in a land far, far away.'

And with that, Ryanair flight 9853 to Cork is gone.

***

I find the Regus Express, pay for a shower (because I wish to be clean for Harvey) and inspect the facilities. They really are fantastic. 'Regus', of course, is Latin for 'kings', and you really can imagine the facility populated by historical monarchs from days gone by – Henry VIII gorging himself on the free tea and coffee, King Arthur booking a meeting room with a round table, King John using the state-of-the-art 'document station' to scan, copy and print copies of the Magna Carta, and Richard III just logging on to the Wi-Fi.[114]

And with that, it's time to head to Arrivals. Harvey's plane from Nice isn't due until 8 p.m., but I want to be there by 6 because it's quite windy today and I know that can reduce flight times.

I stand by the taxi drivers with their little cardboard signs. Some of the more hi-tech guys have got mini-whiteboards they just wipe clean after each job. It's a neat solution and must save them a small fortune in cardboard costs. I decide to have a bit of banter with them.

'Come on, boys, don't be tight, give us one of your whiteboards!'

They laugh along politely but I do actually want one of their whiteboards. If Harvey can't spot me among the Arrivals melee we won't be able to talk turkey (Harvey loves turkey). Worse, we won't be able to talk about my potential TV show either. I've seen whiteboards identical to these for £2.99 on eBay but next-day delivery isn't going to help me now, and that's why I'm more than happy to pay the slightly inflated asking price of Atif, a driver from Premiere Cars (he looks like an Asian Alan Sugar but is better at growing a beard).

---

114 Can't think of anything historical/office-based for him.

As I search for a pen for my £50 whiteboard, there's a sudden tap on my shoulder. I spin round, swivelling on the ball of my foot so as to avoid putting any pressure on my still-throbbing heel injury. It's *DIY SOS*'s Nick Knowles, who comes to Gatwick Airport most evenings to drink, shop and eat.

'Partridge!' he says as he slaps my back.

'Ha!' I laugh, not because it's funny (it isn't, it really hurts) but because I've always been afraid of Nick. He's a big man with a craggy face and an ease among labourers and trades-men that suggests, if the mood took him, he could summon them like Tarzan summons the animals and have them take you to pieces, violence-wise.

'Fuck are you doing here?'

'Nothing, I'm just following in the footsteps of my father.'

'I wondered why you were mincing like that.'

'Ha ha, lovely. No, Dad wasn't gay. Or else I'd still be just a twinkle in his testes. Besides, I wasn't mincing. I was redistributing my weight to protect a heel gash.'

He looks at me. He really is a big chap. And his accent is a guttural East End oi-oi that screams 'I am a physically violent man.'

I carry on: 'And, as I say, I'm on a personal journey to honour the memory of my late father. I'm just here to check out the biz lounge and have a quick word with someone.'

'Who?' (Actually, 'oo?)

'He's not here yet . . .'

'I'll wait with you. Let's have a drink.'

Nick leads the way to the Beehive, a Wetherspoons pub

'with views of Arrivals', and orders a quick pint of lager for us both.

***

What happens next is disappointing for everyone involved. Nick and I have two to three pints of lager. Nick says it will relax me and insists that he only ever presents *DIY SOS* if he's 'DIY S.L.O.S.H.E.D'.

In the event, my dehydration, tiredness and – let's be honest – inexperience with lager as a drink leads me rapidly into a world of very intense intoxication, a fact I only grasp when I spot Mr Kennedy and try to stumble from my bar stool towards him.

I reiterate my desire (and Brian's desire) for filming of my walk to begin ASAP, even suggesting it's my father's desire too, despite him being long-term dead. Ever the salesman, I go on to tell Harvey that, alongside Bradbury, Balding and Portillo, I believe I can become the fourth jewel in his crown, although it seems that, as a result of lager, I actually say 'the fourth jew in his crowd'.

It's at this point that my slick, if slightly loud, sales pitch is stopped in its tracks by Harvey placing a kindly hand on my shoulder (I should stress that the hand is one of his own). I instantly feel sick. I've misread the signals.

It would be unedifying for me to go into too much detail over what happened next, but if you google Oliver Reed's impromptu performance of 'Wild Thing' on Michael Aspel's chat show, I'm told that it was almost exactly like that, down to the choice of song.

I don't know why I felt it would be savvy of me to sing

to the man instead of presenting my ideas in spoken form as rehearsed repeatedly on the hundred-odd miles from my Tilbury Turnback. But that's what I did and that's what I must now live with.

Harvey, I'm told, tried to politely demur, suggesting we talk about it at a later date.

'WE WILL TALK ABOUT IT NOW, MR NICH-OLS!' I told him, temporarily mistaking the TV agent for the high-end chain of department stores.

When he pushed past me, I screamed at my co-drinker, 'PLANT ONE ON HIM, KNOWLESY! LAY HIM OUT!'

But Knowlesy didn't plant one on him or lay him out. Instead he pretended he wasn't with me. But that's Nick for you. He's basically a big horrible git of a man.

27.

'PON THE WINGS OF
A CHILD

***

IN A PRETTY CRUMMY mood today. Think I might get a tattoo. It'll be on my forehead and it'll say, 'Why do I bother?'

It's the morning after the night before this morning and I'm sitting in a branch of Ready to Munch (known by the French as *Pret a Munger*). It's the one in Gatwick Airport, which tells you that I'm still in Gatwick Airport. It's not important how long I've been here, but I guess if this were a film they'd have done that thing where I stay still while everyone around me moves unbelievably quickly.

Most people choose not to linger in a place like this. But I feel a bit like Tom Hanks in *The Terminal*, only without the

Russian accent that, hand on heart, I think Tom knows he never really mastered.

But yeah, feeling pretty piddled off, to be fair. Then again, so would you be if you'd just voluntarily taken a four-day detour on the basis of assurances given to you by a business associate who then failed to make good on them. Call it re-neging, call it welshing, you just don't bloody do that.

But it's not all doom and gloom. My foot's still horribly painful but I did spend the night in Gatwick's wonderful Ibis Hotel (worth every one of its two stars). And, after a Grolschy sleep, I awoke and gave my last pair of function-ing underpants a much-needed sink wash. With no wash-ing powder per se, I improvised with a splodge of Head & Shoulders.

The results were impressive. Admittedly, they were never going to come out spotless, but what I can say is that there was a genuine improvement in terms of both stains *and* stench.[115] And because this branch of Ready to Munch is quite warm, there's every chance that in another couple of hours my pants will be genuinely dry.

And then what? I look at the table before me and imagine the tray is a map of southern England. Norwich is the empty

---

115 I actually believe Head & Shoulders is a bit of a misnomer. The 'Head' bit's fine. Most of us have hair on our heads and we like to keep it clean. But other than Richard Keys, there are very few men out there who have so much hair on their shoulders that it needs to be sham-pooed. (Richard even blow-dries his.) Around a man's privates, however, it's a very different issue. I'm no branding expert but surely a better name would have been Head & Groins?

sachet of pepper, Dungeness the dirty cardboard coffee cup. Which means I'll have to be the limp bit of lettuce. But that's OK. I kinda feel like one! I position them crudely into an approximate geography around the half-eaten bagel that is London and look at how far I've come. A long way, that's how far. And that's something to be proud of. You could say I've already honoured my late father. Does it really matter if I walk all the way from pepper sachet to coffee cup? This isn't *SAS: Are You Tough Enough?* Who'll even know? Anyway, just a thought! And I sit there a while longer.

My phone begins to ring. Indeed keeps ringing until I answer it.

It's my assistant and she sounds excited. Which is all I need.

'Let me guess,' I say. 'That man at church smiled at you again?'

But she tells me, 'No,' and starts talking about read receipts, one of the few things that still gets her excited. For some reason, this primitive means of knowing who's opened an email you've sent absolutely beguiles her. But then she's only just got over 1471. She says she sent an email about my walk and she's received read receipts back from loads of them. Everyone's reading about it.

'[My assistant],' I say. 'Calm down. Who's everyone?'

'Everyone. Loads of people. Gary Wilmot.'

'OK.'

'Sue Cook.'

'OK.'

'Dale Winton.'

'OK.'

'Ainsley Harriott.'

'OK. Julia Bradbury?'

'No.'

'OK.'

'Phillip Schofield.'

'OK.'

'And Eamonn Holmes.'

'Right. Actually, can you say those again?'

'Gary Wilmot.'

'OK.'

'Sue Cook.'

'OK.'

'Dale Winton.'

'OK.'

'Ainsley Harriott.'

'OK. Julia Bradbury?'

'No.'

'OK.'

'Phillip Schofield.'

'OK.'

'And Eamonn Holmes.'

'OK. Right.'

There's a pregnant pause, although I generally try to avoid using the word 'pregnant' in relation to my assistant because she's sixty-nine and Baptist. I find myself pinching the bridge of my nose.

She asks why I'm sighing and I inform her that it wasn't a sigh, it was just decisive exhaling.

'So they all know I'm doing it?' I say, just so I know. 'And they'll all know [when] I finish the walk?'

'"If"? What do you mean, "if"? Are you not going to finish the walk?'

'I didn't say "if,"' I tell her. 'I said "when".'

Which is true. And if you look up four lines, you'll see quite clearly that I said 'when'.

'So you are going to finish the walk?' she asks.

And I tell her, 'Yes, of course I am!' Why wouldn't I? Just because I sit in a coffee shop for six hours doesn't mean I've lost my sense of purpose. She's unbelievable! She adds that it'd be a bit embarrassing if I did pull out now that people are taking an interest, and I hang up on her – in a good mood. Yes, a very good mood. This is all great.

And with that, I gobble off the last of my yoghurt-covered cranberries like a druggy bingeing on a fresh batch of ecstasy pellets, gather up my things and head off.

***

Well, my assistant was in the right ballpark to suggest that my walk has the capacity to capture people's imaginations. Although this afternoon it's not people I'm joined by, it's *children*.

In the ballad she did that wasn't by Dolly Parton (don't remember name), Whitney Houston sang: 'I believe the children are our future.' I also believe that and applaud Houston for articulating what many other high-profile media figures, such as Pat Sharp, do not.

So you can imagine my glee when I find myself flanked, quite unprompted, by some giddy kiddies.

Their timing is something special. I'm still dwelling on the whole Gatwick debacle but am now given fresh impetus by the sudden presence of chatting, laughing, vital children.

The road and pavement are suddenly awash with these little people, teeming around like maggots on a carcass (me being the carcass). I tower over them like a farmer wading through a country lane jammed with sheep, but, crucially, I am being propelled onwards, carried on the wings of children's laughter (metaphorically).

A quick check of my map tells me that just seventy miles separate me and Dungeness nuclear power station, the place my father so very nearly reached. And now, fuelled by nothing other than pure kiddy power, I intend to enjoy every last one them.

I spy their carer. It transpires that these children are from a local primary school. They have heard about my fundraising efforts for 'Alvin's Foundation' and were moved to come and see me, having been informed of my whereabouts by a nosey governor who spotted me leaving Gatwick. They also raise money for a leukaemia charity so were keen to come along and show their support.

They are all around me and I feel quite messianic. I am Muhammad Ali in Kinshasa, I am Jacko at the Brits, I am Indiana Jones after leaving the Temple of Doom, a Partridgean Pied Piper piping his pipe.

To some broadcasters of my age and gender, this would give rise to a certain . . . [I pause to remove my spectacles, pinch the bridge of my nose between finger and thumb and carefully choose the correct word] . . . awkwardness. We live in a post-Yewtree age.

Now, this is an uncomfortable thing to discuss, but I run towards discomfort like a man who has strapped truth explosives to his body and made his peace with God. And I'm saying that broadcasters are now deeply, deeply wary of any interaction with children.

Some of our Sunday Skype Clubs[116] have been given over to discussing this very issue. We hurl in scenarios and the group debates whether they should be red-flagged. Is it OK to hug a crying child? All right, what if the child is fifteen and a girl? Or if this takes place in your dressing room and you've taken wine? Or if the child's parents are present but temporarily distracted? Or if the child needs help applying a thigh bandage and only then do you see she's wearing lipstick? And the thigh bandage is made out of lace and looks more like a frilly garter? Or the child isn't upset but you're trampolining together and the kid does a brilliant somersault after weeks of trying and you realise all he/she wants is a 'well done' and a pat on the back? Or the child is a chimney sweep and has become lodged in your chimney and is asking, no, *pleading* for you to grab him by the legs and pull him down, and his parents aren't present and you're only wearing shorts because it's hot? Admittedly, some of these questions are better and more relevant than others – not all

---

116 The Sunday Skype Club is a weekly video-call social – usually taking place when *Sunday Politics* comes on and Eamonn (Holmes) has finished his breakfast – in which me, Eamonn (Holmes), John Stapleton (when allowed), Pete Sissons and a Hairy Biker meet up to shoot the breeze, tackle the issues of the day and slag off other broadcasters. It's become less and less frequent as Eamonn (Holmes) has started to do it from the bath, which hasn't gone down well. It's not his flesh – the bubble bath covers that – so much as the fact that he'll be eating sliders while he chats to us (they're basically small burgers). With the suds on his face, he's like Santa playing *Pac-Man*.

of them are mine – but it shows how seriously we take the issue, and the legal minefield we're now dealing with. The Hairy Biker tends not to join in, claiming, 'It's not difficult, just don't touch up kids.' But that strikes me as incredibly simplistic. I've seen broadcasters – good men, good presenters – almost paralysed in the presence of children. I, thank God, am not one of them and am able to enjoy the simple company of kids, such as now, on this walk.

We all walk together, me responding to their questions with trademark kindliness. Yes, I am famous. No, I'm not from *Britain's Got Talent*. No, I don't have sandwiches. Yes, I like sandwiches. My favourite sandwich filling is tuna. Tuna is a fish. No, Nemo is not a tuna. No, I don't know what Nemo is. Yes, he is definitely a fish. Yes, I like *Finding Nemo*. No, not all fish talk. If I could be a fish I would be a trout.

And all on the move. These kids must be fighting fit because my pace doesn't slacken and they're able to keep up with me.

But then, I reason, children have moved on from the consumptive, wheezing specimens of yesteryear – the ones from Dickens books (not the films, since they tend to be the plump public school children who populate theatre groups).

Of course, children can be *too* fit. I'm thinking here of the butch cherubs you see on religious frescoes. It's a good thing they're heavenly creatures because – and I might have thought about this too much – if they did turn on you, they could quickly overpower and pummel you.[117]

---

117 My own son was a much thinner baby. We took him to the doctor because he had a concave chest but they wouldn't treat it. They said he was just puny.

Fascinatingly muscular physiques they have, though. Understandable, if you think about it. From a biomechanics point of view, cherubs are going to need considerable strength to stay airborne. Assuming they weigh a couple of stone and can't generate much speed on take-off, most of that lift is going to be vertical.

Then I guess it's up to the cherubs to observe some basic safety protocols in mid-air. A chilling thought. Cherubs are essentially twelve-month-old babies with wings. Difficult enough to control at that age, but if they could fly . . .! And don't get me started on Cupid! Giving a baby a bow and arrow is just rank stupidity, or 'cupidity'. Different times, of course . . .

Yes, these children are impressively fleet of foot and a credit to whichever primary school[118] they hail from. But

---

118 Or should I say academy! The government has been trying to turn failing schools (aka 'state schools') into academies, or it might be free schools, for some time now. And while no one really knows what this means or how a school differs from an academy, or indeed a free school, it's a move that has been vehemently opposed by teachers. And that's good enough for me! I try as far as possible to keep my radio show apolitical but teachers really are blithering scum, and whatever they disagree with, I agree with.

I was convinced of this after lunching a couple of years ago with writer/broadcaster/agitator Toby Young. He blew me *away* with his vision for Britain's schools and, on his advice, I created a weekly feature on my show called 'Shame on Them, Shame on Them', in which we singled out an unorthodox teacher and gave out his or her name and address on air. We were soon instructed to cease this segment, but it still felt thrilling to be improving the lives of young people and effecting real change in our education system.

their close attendance soon begins to wear thin. They buffet me in a playful way, as kids do, but continue to do so long after it's stopped being funny. And even though I've kept my sarcasm quite rudimentary for their benefit – 'Oh, you nudged me again. How original! What a brilliant thing to do! I wish I were as funny as you, etc., etc.' – they take each utterance at face value and can't grasp for a second that I'm getting razzed off. Eventually, I've had enough. I suggest that they see which of them can make it to the letterbox first and they race towards it, teacher and all, not realising that my route takes me right and I duck off at a delicious right angle, helping myself to the packed lunch I'd agreed to look after[119] as I walk away.

***

By the end of the day I have reached East Grinstead. I'm almost certain there's no 'West' Grinstead, so it makes no sense that this place should be called East Grinstead. I try to

---

Toby knows what's what and is able to give genuinely balanced political commentary by virtue of having once been of the opposing political persuasion. That means he can claim to see the whole spectrum before deciding that the right-wing option is better – so he can never be accused of partisanship. Other columnists are incredibly partisan and automatically favour one side of the debate. But if you've supported both in your time, even if you only ever wore the political colours of the team you hate as a short-lived tactical ploy, you can dodge this accusation and quite reasonably claim to see the whole picture, scoffing at the folly of your opponents in a 'Ha, yes, I was once that naive' kind of way.
119 Egg and cress.

put this out of my mind but, quite understandably, am only partially successful.[120]

I spend the night at the Lark Guesthouse, run by Dave and Ashley Lambert. They're a gay couple, so their sense of humour's not for me, but they're welcoming and we get to chatting about the town. I notice that they have a habit of finishing each other's sentences. At first I find it endearing, but it quickly becomes incredibly annoying. I zone out for about fifty minutes, and when I come to I realise they've been talking about caravanning the entire time. I start to wonder if it might be a gay sex term that Dale Winton failed to include in the glossary he did for me. Yet it turns out to be anything but – they're just keen caravanners – so I have absolutely no reason to worry.

What I'm really interested in, however, is Scientology. The kooky religion has its UK headquarters here and, given that they're long-term residents of the town, I figure Dave and Ashley can give me the inside line on what goes on in the Scientology compound. I'm wrong, though. Possibly fearing for their safety if any less-than-positive words end up in this book, I can't get a single thing out of the otherwise-hospitable

---

120 Subsequent research by my publisher revealed that there is actually a West Grinstead. More embarrassing still, West Grinstead includes the growing village of Partridge Green, a shade I once tried to have added to the official Dulux colour palette. Interestingly, the town is just a stone's throw from the north slope of the South Downs, surely one of the Downs' premier slopes.

queens.[121] I, on the other hand, have no such worries and am more than happy to give my own critique. As I see it █████

████████████████████████████████

████████████████████████████████

██████████████████████ and that's just for starters. ████

████████████████████████████████

███████████████████████████████ at every bath time apparently.

████ other ████████████████████

████████████████████████████████

████████████████████████ Aldi. █████

██████████████

████████████████████████████████

████████████ tactical firearms team ████████

████████████████████████████████

████████████████████████████████

█████████████ needless to say, █████ last laugh.

With my injured foot now throbbing like some sort of weird percussion instrument, I bed down and sleep a deep, if slightly fevered, sleep.

***

When I wake my sheets are sodden with perspiration – like, *sodden* – and I become concerned that the staff might think Partridge has peed himself. After showering and dressing, I decide to leave the cleaner [Dave] a sweetly rhyming note

---

121 I was unsure whether this term was acceptable so ran it past a pub landlord I know who used to be gay and he assured me that it was absolutely fine.

explaining 'I'm a bad *sweater*, not a bed *wetter*!' before leaving the room.

No sooner have I done so than I realise – oh thump a chump! – I've left my jumper on the bed, and the note might sound like it's on behalf of the pullover. I try to open the door but I've left my key on the bureau and can't gain access to the room. It's a truly terrible moment.

Leaving East Grinny, I'm struck once again by how different the world would have looked in my father's time. There are no specific examples of that at the moment because I'm walking past some oak trees and they would have looked exactly the same,[122] but I'm struck by how different the world would have looked nevertheless. Because it really would have looked different. Yes, quite, quite different.

I pass the Queen Victoria Hospital and briefly wonder whether I should pop in to get my foot looked at (it now hurts a great, great deal multiplied by a million). But then I rethink. Going to casualty for a cut foot? Dear, oh dear, how *would* I have coped in Vietnam? Anyway, with the exception of light bulbs, hymens,[123] and my heart – which has been broken into a million pieces by a woman called Angela – everything's fixable. I miss Angela.

---

122 What a pointless tree.

123 This is known as an Oxford comma. Thank you.

28.

MY ANGEL(A)

***

ONE OF THE THINGS I love most about receptionists is that they have to be nice to you. The same is true of waitresses and barmaids, although masseuses don't seem to have got the memo.

It's vital that members of these professions – often women, but it's also now legal for men – smile warmly and show a keen interest in what you did at the weekend. Of course, if they're not up to this, nobody will mind and they can go and find themselves another job. Not willing to go quietly? No problem. A quiet word with the office manager from one of the more senior members of staff should see them being shown the door within twenty-four hours.

Thankfully, there were no such issues with Angela. I'll never forget the day we met. Not literally (can't remember date), but more in the general sense that she would come to assume a prominent role in my life. But also in the life of the radio station. We'd had to let six receptionists go in little more than a year, and what the front desk badly needed was a period of stability.

Right from the start Angela just 'got' my sense of humour. She 'got' where my humour was coming from and she 'got' what I was trying to achieve with it. Some of my stuff can be pretty out there,[124] and I know our previous few receptionists had struggled to tune in to it, but not Angela. There wasn't just chemistry between us, there was physics too.

Hers wasn't an obvious kind of beauty, and I liked that. You had to put in a bit of effort to spot it, particularly if she'd had a couple of snifters the night before. But take your time, be prepared to look at her from a wide range of angles, and you would eventually strike gold. Not that I'm an oil painting myself. I'm a middle-aged man who is acutely aware of his own physical imperfections. I may have genuinely world-class hair and a genuinely world-class way of styling it, but in other ways (e.g. fat back) I'm far from a perfect specimen.

So it's just as well that there's more to love than giving someone an arbitrary mark out of ten for how attractive they are. So what if I was a six and she was an eight? Or if *I* was an eight and *she* was a six (which is what it was)? Far more significant is the complex interplay of a whole range

---

124 Think 'Richard Hammond', but more so.

of intangibles, from pheromones to personality to hygiene (the ladies I date *must* be clean).

The first time I ever tongue-shagged Angela (i.e. kissed her) was when we were both being held hostage by DJ-gone-berserk Pat Farrell. That may seem counter-intuitive, but when you're staring death in the face it can make you profoundly randy.

Twenty-four hours later the siege was over, miraculously without a single casualty.[125] So in the weeks that followed, Angela and I were free to take our relationship to the next level, away from the glare of the world's media and a sad Irishman with a shotgun. It was a chance we seized with both of our four hands.

We progressed from gentle kissing to heavy petting in, what, six days? Sure, there were moments when we'd get a bit handy with each other, but generally it was a phase dominated by lots and lots of snogging. Now, when you've been snogging as long as I have, you get a pretty good feel for the strengths and weaknesses of your technique. Personally, I'm a fairly accomplished all-rounder, as comfortable nibbling a lip as I am when the mouths go wide. Meanwhile, regular Murray Minting means my breath is *always* in great condition.

My one flaw – other than dribbling – is that during standing-up snogs I have a tendency to over-lean. On first dates, when the woman's not been briefed, this will usually mean she's forced backwards and onto the floor. But in later dates, with everything now out in the open, a wall or bus

---

125 With the exception of Michael, who died.

shelter is usually sufficient as a backstop. In my twenties I worried that this tendency on my part may have come across as slightly 'forward' or 'predatory'. But as I've got older I've come to accept that this loss of balance is more likely a problem with my inner ear.

It'd be an exaggeration to say that Angela and I kissed for days at a time, but snogs of between eight and ten minutes certainly weren't unusual. I'm a keen stats man so I made it my business to time our kisses and jot the results down in a notebook. It made for fascinating reading. She tended to be the one to end the snogs (Angela wasn't a very good nose-breather), with our briefest normally in the morning before I'd brushed my teeth, and our longest either on the occasions we'd stop in a layby on the way home or when she was leathered.

The fact that we worked in the same building meant we were able to see lots of each other, and Frenchie sessions would often take place during my show. The best time was after I'd thrown to the lunchtime news when we had about fourteen minutes to really go at it. Simon would often be in the studio with us, but it wasn't a problem because he had his magazines.

Post-snog, we'd typically find ourselves extremely hungry, and Simon would be dispatched to get us a nice salad from McDonald's. With the studio to ourselves Angela would discuss the key elements of the snog – 'I liked how your kept licking the roof of my mouth' or whatever – and I would just listen quietly and stare at her.

Of course, the next stage was outright sex. And while I'm not prepared to go into detail out of respect for Angela, suffice it to say she was strong and she had stamina.

She also had a remarkable appetite, not something you'd necessarily expect from a forty-four-year-old who shops at Etam. And while I'm no prude – far from it, I find sex *extremely* pleasant – for a while I actually thought there was something wrong with her. I went back to my Blu-ray collection and rewatched the film where Michael Fastbender plays a fuckaholic, but concluded that what Angela was feeling was perfectly normal. At the end of the day, the explanation was simple: I just turned her on.

***

After ten days of dating, Angela and I moved in together. Some people thought that was a bit quick, but it wasn't and they were wrong. I suggested we cohabit at my place, Denton Abbey. It's one of Norwich's marquee residential properties and brilliant in every way. But she didn't want to.

'All right, then, I'll move in to your place if that's what you'd prefer, Sparrow.' (Sparrow is the name I would call her when we were making love.)

'OK, Big Bird.' (And Big Bird is the name she would call me.)

'Don't get me wrong, I still think Dent Ab could work' – I tended to be quite a chatty lover – 'but at the end of the day you're making the final decision and I'm 100 per cent comfortable with that.'

'Uh-huh.' Angela tended to be less chatty. She might respond to the odd thing, but as a general rule, once love-making had begun in anger, she preferred not to be disturbed. And I was fine with that. A lot of my utterances didn't require a response anyway; often they were just reminders or items on my to-do list.

The reason she wanted me to move in to her house was her kids. Colby (fifteen) and Phillip (I want to say twelve?) were Angela's children from her first marriage. With their father largely absent, theirs had been a topsy-turvy childhood, and Angela was keen not to inflict a house move on them, even into, like I say, one of Norwich's marquee residential properties.

They were basically good kids. Quite different – Phillip was short, Colby had spots[126] – but I had a lot of time for them. I'd raised a couple of teenagers of my own so I knew more or less what to expect, but Colby and Phillip were different. Admittedly, they didn't answer back to their mum and had never been in trouble at school, but the fact remained that they *were* from a broken home. Statistically, that meant the chances of them ending up as skag heads were sky-high. And I couldn't let this happen.

Of course, hindsight is a wonderful thing, and looking back I can see I might have gone in too hard. I've never believed in rules for the sake of rules, but I did feel it was important they washed their hands before dinner, went into the garden if they needed to break wind and were in their jim-jams by 8 p.m.[127] I also requested that they say grace before each meal (as an atheist I wasn't bound by this and could begin eating as soon as I sat down), and finally that I,

---

126 And how!

127 Angela had no problem making love to me when the boys were still awake, but I was less keen.

and I alone, had dominion over the remote control.

It was in about week four that things started to break down. I noticed Colby, his poor face pebble-dashed with pimples,[128] had been exchanging glances with his mother over dinner. I sensed that it was time Angela and I had a chat.

'So listen, I wanna get things out in the open. I noticed you and Colbs looking at each other earlier. Is everything OK, Sparrow?'

(I had decided to wait until the boys had gone to bed.)

'Too strict.'

'Got it. Actually had a hunch it might be something like that. But listen, that's cool with Big Bird, I'll just change tack. Maybe the guys need a bit more carrot and a bit less stick. What d'you reckon?'

'Ooh.'

Changing tack was a decision that would change everything. I accepted that no matter how hard I tried, I would never be their father. Yes, by easing off on the boys there would be nothing to stop them sliding into a life of drug addiction and petty crime, but ultimately that would be on their dad.

Instead, I became a kind of best buddy to the boys, taking them out for long afternoons bird-watching or to the miniature steam railway.[129] They'd often say it was boring and they didn't want to go, but teenagers speak in opposites, remember, so I knew this was just their way of thanking me. I even agreed that when Colby turned sixteen he'd be allowed

---

128 In all honesty it looked more like a crumpet than a face.

129 The 'miniature' is a reference to the trains, not the steam.

to sit in the passenger seat, on a trial basis and provided the journey was short. It's what I liked to describe as Step-Dadding 2.0.

But the good times were not to last.

***

'I want to play your bum like the bongos.' It was the most foolish text message I had ever sent. I'd been out to a work do at the local swimming baths. Normally, we'd just go to the pub and have a few drinks, but it was my turn to organise this one and I felt people would benefit from doing something different for a change.

What I'd forgotten was that Angela can't swim. She'd had lessons as a child but she said she just kept sinking all the time. I was keen as Colman's not to exclude her, though, so I suggested she come along and stand in the shallow end. It was an idea that did not find favour.

I felt a bit blue going on a night out without my Ange, but to my surprise the evening was a roaring success. Only four of us made it in the end, just slightly shy of the sixteen who said they'd come. But that actually worked to our advantage – I happened to have brought along four juice boxes, so after our swim I invited the guys to sit in my car and drink them.

I got on particularly well with Melanie, a woman from Accounts, and got home to find she'd texted me a picture of herself wearing a dressing gown that was slightly ajar. Anyway, we exchanged a few texts, and it was when Angela saw the one from me that said 'I'd like to play your bum like the bongos' that our relationship collapsed and she kicked me out of the house.

I tried to explain to her that it was just random banter between workmates, that there was nothing going on between us and I could just have easily sent those texts to a man, but Angela was having none of it as she can be quite stubborn.

All in all it was a sequence of events that would lead me to have a breakdown live on air and be suspended from my post for two weeks. But every cloud is said to have a lining of precious metal (typically silver), and in this case the time off allowed me to go for broke and tick off an item on my bucket list – a three-day watercolour break on the banks of Loch Lomond (during which I listened to 'Hold Me Close' by David Essex, on loop).[130]

As for Angela, I still see her occasionally, not least at work every single day. She doesn't really talk to me, but I understand that and wouldn't dream of having her sacked for insubordination.

I did toy with the idea of sending her a message in this book but my publisher felt it would be inappropriate and

---

130 Odd because this is the song to which I fell in love with my ex-wife Carol. She'd told me (in confidence) that love-making made her scalp sweat, so in the early days of our courtship I'd treat her to a post-coital hair brush. We'd sit naked on the bed with me combing her locks for bits that had become damp and tangled. This was the record we listened to. Years later, David bought a static home from me and tried to get money off because he didn't like the colour. I relented because he intimidates me, always has. I may be wrong about this, but I'm reliably informed that he once tried to put a curse on Leo Sayer after an argument over the bill in an Indian restaurant. David still has the static home but doesn't live in it. Having recently become an eBay powerseller of Japanese car parts, he uses it to keep stock in these days.

I agreed. After all, even if I did still have feelings for her, and that's not something I'm prepared to discuss publicly, would this really be the forum in which to say, 'Angela, if you're reading this, please talk to me when I walk past you at reception. I always try to catch your eye but you just look down as if you're reading something, even though I know you're not'?

Of course it wouldn't. Ditto something like, 'I know I made a mistake and I know you said you've moved on, but I love you and I need you and I swear on the life of my children (and yours!) that I do not want to play that woman's bum like the bongos.'

No, like I say, anything in that vein that would be crossing a line. Best to keep my own counsel.

But, while I think of it, one other thing I wouldn't have my publishers print is a quick sign-off along the lines of, 'I think about you all the time: how your nose wiggles when you laugh; how you go blotchy after a hot shower. I just want to touch you, smell you, hold you tight in the pouring rain. You complete me, babygirl x'[131]

---

131 Call me.

29.

HARD SHOULDER,
SORE FOOT

***

YOU REJOIN ME A few days later, and what a few days they've been! I've enjoyed some of the finest strolling of my career, taking my time to really *revel* in the act of walking – genuinely pleased that boomeranging my way around London has gifted my 160-mile route an additional 120 miles of sheer pleasantness.[132]

Admittedly, the pace has slackened a touch due to my maimed foot, dropping from around twenty miles a day to fewer than five. (Yep, I can state I've a sedate gait of late!)

---

132 Besides, 280 miles is still more than manageable. If you walked into the sky for 280 miles, you'd almost reach a weather satellite.

But this gentle trundle has allowed me to take in the sassy majesty of this land we call Britain. After all, I tell myself, when Wordsworth 'wandered lonely as a cloud' he was talking about the low-hanging cumulus clouds that achieve relatively low speeds, rather than the higher-altitude cirrus clouds that I'm told can hit 100mph if pushed along by the jet stream.

One night saw me drop anchor in Royal Tunbridge Wells, after a steady five miler. For those who've never visited, RoyTunWel is an absolute peach of a town, and great value for its Royal moniker. The last of the working classes were driven out some time in the late 1960s, and you can really sense that feeling of safety as you limp along the high street.[133]

The following night's stop was just three miles down the road. I holed up at Tricklebrook Fishery. It wasn't ideal – doesn't have any bedrooms and was also shut – but I was on a country road with no sign of any hotels. I could probably have found somewhere if I'd kept going for an hour or so, but my foot had other ideas so I had a little lie down in the doorway.

There was no one around, so after a quick snooze I went over to one of the carp ponds and stuck my foot in. I once

---

133 By way of a side note, I've long argued that the Windsors should rename Norwich as Royal Norwich. Not just because of the city's fine architecture and storied history, but because of our blind devotion to the crown. Bad-mouth the monarchy in front of a citizen of Norwich and, even if that citizen is a woman, you'll be leaving town with a thick ear.

saw a documentary where some fish ate the infection off a guy's foot. Or was it dead skin? Either way, the carp gave me a wide berth. Maybe they were just frigid, if that's the right word.

And now, I'm on the road again, at the approximate speed of a kerb-crawler down an industrial road behind a train station.

Yes, it's been a slow few days but I've enjoyed myself immensely, despite the admittedly incessant throb of my swelling foot. And I'm now just fifty miles from the reactor at Dungeness 'A' power station, and I can almost feel the air starting to get . . . I want to say 'nuclear'?

***

Walking past a white van in serious need of a jet wash and an Air Wick, I hear, wafting from its passenger window, the unmistakeable sound of 'The Chain' by Fleetwood Mac, once the theme music to the BBC's Formula One motor racing coverage.[134] The song ends and I'm treated to a few seconds of local-radio disc jockeying from, well, I forget the name of the station, but you can tell by the smile in the DJ's voice that it's one of those whose name sounds like a panty liner: Dream or Breeze or Shape or Silk or something.

Oh, and this guy? He is having an absolute '*mare*, a real genocide of a show. He mis-speaks the band name – Meetwood Flac! – throws to the news when the news isn't ready, does the classic 'Janice on line one, sorry, line two; actually,

---

134 Before Sky got hold of it and made it so stat-heavy that the screen resembles the 'mix' option of Ceefax.

is it Janet?' and develops a dry mouth so that his lips become coated with that creamy saliva that makes them give off a gentle 'clit, clit, clit'[135] sound as he speaks. It's a joy to listen to and reminds me of the time I let my then-teenage Denise come to Radio Norwich for the day and, for a bit of work experience, helm a phone-in on same-sex marriage. She struggled to calm an irate Catholic and basically went to pieces. I later informed her that she'd never been on air (and the Catholic was an actor friend of mine), which seemed to upset her more, if anything, but I'd felt it important to show her that live radio's not as easy as her school friends seemed to think and perhaps she should ask them to show a little more respect when they're next round.

But it's while delighting in this man's very obvious radio collapse (or obvious to me, anyway) that I remember something. I've totally forgotten about work. It's Saturday tea time and I need to be back behind the mic by 10 a.m. on Monday. My listeners have been in the hands of Dave Clifton for two weeks now, and I know for a fact that his schtick will be wearing seriously thin.

I'm going to have to seriously up my pace. Yes, if I'm to reach to my destination – and I'm not just saying this to set up a dramatic finale for my book – what follows will be the greatest achievement of my life.

***

---

135 I know 'clit' has another meaning but I don't know how better to describe it.

I indicate right and head down the slip road. I'm not in a car, by the way. I've just figured out that my quickest route to the coast is going to be the M20. (When I said 'indicate right' that was just me using my arm as an indicator.)

I'm totally in the zone now. Need to be. Have to be. Am. I owe it to my dad. It'd be pretty swell if my foot would cut me some slack, but you can't have it all, right? I took my sock off to have a look earlier and it made for pretty interesting viewing. I wouldn't say the foot's ballooned – it's not ballooned – but it's definitely put on a bit of weight. Still, happens to the best of us. You want to see my back!

No, but seriously, it's definitely become infected – whether from the stick that cut it or the damp old bread that I found in the park, I know not. What I do know is that it's swollen and emitting a kind of yellow gel (I guess you could call it 'foot tripe'), while – and this might be my imagination – audibly humming with germs. If it gets any more painful, I'm going to have to hop!

***

The lorries are honking at me quite a bit now. I can't tell if it's because you don't normally see people on the hard shoulder when it's gone midnight or because I'm hopping.

Still, credit where credit's due – it's a lovely motorway. Loud, mind you. Jesus. It was quieter at Gatwick.

Zoush!
Zoush!
Meeow![136]

---

136 That one was a motorbike, not a cat.

Zoush!

It's a bit demoralising but I try to stay positive. It may *seem* like these vehicles will beat me to the coast, but what if they don't? Who's to say I won't reel them in? It happened in the story of the Tortoise and the Hare. Then again, the tortoise didn't have a gammy foot.

I check the wound again. I know this sounds weird but I swear it's developed its own pulse. A rhythmic throb that seems for all the world to be spelling 'Help. Antibiotics' in Morse code. But I might be wrong about that.

***

Junction 9, and I've reached Ashford in Kent. I'm no longer hopping but it's dark, and without a high-vis jacket I'm more or less invisible. I find a cat's eye – not a real one, or at least I don't think it is – and try to wedge it into my back pocket. My hope is that it will balance there and be picked up by the headlights of the onrushing traffic. No such luck; it keeps falling to the floor. With my hands otherwise engaged – I'm in the grip of a fever now so am carrying my coat, jumper and shirt – I have no other way to protect myself than to walk backwards with the cat's eye in my mouth. It's uncomfortable and tastes of carriageway.

***

Right. I think I've got muddled up because I appear to be inside the Channel Tunnel. Yep. I am inside the Channel Tunnel.

Not a trillion per cent sure how this happened. But it has. Just tracking back. I know I haven't eaten in over a day and the only drink I've had is a bottle of warm apple juice a lorry driver threw out of his window (thank you, whoever you are!). I also know I managed to make it to Folkestone at the end of the M20. Then there are a few blanks.

For a moment there, I thought I'd made it into the main reactor at Dungeness 'A' power station. There's a similar aesthetic – men in high-vis jackets patrolling the vicinity, ceiling strip lights illuminating yellow-and-black hazard signs, the pleasing clack of shoe on concrete echoing around the walls like it does in *Moonraker* – but then I see two men in football shirts eating a Ginsters and it occurs to me that hot food wouldn't be allowed inside a nuclear reactor.

Yes, I've walked up the car entrance of the Channel Tunnel, or Chunnel. Chilling to think how easily I almost trafficked myself. If a man like me can almost smuggle himself cross-border without even intending to, then how piddle-easy must it be to achieve it if you're actually trying?

It's Sunday lunchtime. I should be at the Boxley Wheatsheaf, tucking into a hot beef dinner while chortling through meaty mouthfuls at the wicked wit of local folk group Will o' the Wisp. But I'm not at the Boxley Wheatsheaf. I am 144 furlongs, or eighteen 'miles', from Dungeness.

30.

RISING UP, BACK
ON THE STREET

***

ADVERSITY MAKES YOU LOOK at things differently. There's a video on YouTube called 'The Crawl', which shows the closing stages of the female Ironman [sic] World Championship in 1997.

The two leading ladies, Sian Welch and Wendy Ingraham, are metres from the tape and determined to scoop gold but, after jogging for 100 miles, their legs have other ideas! With the finish line in sight, both sets of legs turn to jelly and the willowy women seemingly take it in turns to collapse before hauling themselves up, carrying on – and collapsing again and again – less than ten yards from glory, before eventually one of them waddles to victory.

I think the video is meant to celebrate the triumph of the human spirit, but good God, it is one of the funniest things I've *ever* seen. A friend of mine took the video and added the theme tune to *Steptoe and Son*, which made me literally howl with laughter.

Well, I'm not laughing now. Now I am those collapsible ladies. My legs are their legs. My torment is their torment, or slightly tougher. *Je suis Sian*. And *#jesuiswendyaussi*. I am overcome by an intense feeling of shame, not just for laughing at these formidable women, but for emailing the Steptoed vid to everyone in my address book.

They were trying. Did it really matter who won the 1997 female Ironman [sic] World Championship? Of course not. It's almost literally a non-event. But they pushed themselves anyway. Why? Who knows. Perhaps their fathers had driven that route on the way to a job interview. Perhaps they were coached by bossy husbands like Paula Radcliffe was. Or perhaps they just hated each other and wanted to revel in their vanquished rival's misery.

Whatever the reason, they carried on. Martin Luther King's son, Martin Luther King Jr, once said, 'We've got to keep on keeping on.' I say something similar, and a touch more poetic: 'I've got to not stop not stopping.'

And, somehow, I do not stop not stopping. Is my progress painfully slow? Sure. Is my bloated hiking shoe leaving a trail of gunk behind it like a leather snail? Yes, absolutely. But somehow I move forwards.

My head is dizzy with distress. Buildings, trees and well-wishers swim into vision and then are gone. My thoughts are fleeting, disconnected. Holy *ballbags*, my foot hurts. I walk along the Royal Military Canal on the way into Hythe and wonder what makes a canal 'military', eventually picturing anti-radar gun barges towed by armoured drays.

With the dregs of my phone's battery, I track my progress on Google Maps. It amuses me for a while that this portion of the UK map, when zoomed in, looks like a cat's face in profile.

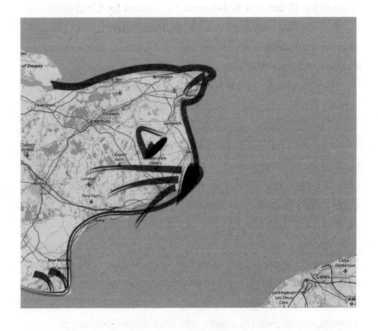

Margate would be the ear, St Margaret's at Cliffe the nose, the concave bit between Folkestone and Dungeness a mouth, wide open as if it's about to eat Calais. Sorry, Calais, but you're about to be breakfast for the Coastal Cat of Kent! I laugh and then laugh some more and realise I can't stop laughing even when I pop into the Jet garage on Dymchurch

Road to buy Rolos. The man behind the counter doesn't flinch, although he refuses to let me have the Rolos when I'm unable to remember my PIN. In the end, I give him my watch and he lets me have the snacks. He probably thinks he's got a good deal, but wait until he realises that he's just been given a snide Rolex from China. (I have a drawer full of them, which I give to workmen as gifts. My real watch is a genuine Rolex – a Submariner, as worn by Connery.)

It's Sunday evening and I continue to trudge southwards through Littlestone, Greatstone and Lade, towards Lydd-on-Sea. I know that I'm close now. In the far distance, I can see the bulky form of Dungeness nuclear power station, squatting on the shore as if it's guarding the British Isles from invaders and is ready to belch hot radiation right in their French faces.

By now, I'm making involuntary noises every other step, the pain forcing a whispered groan from my lips – 'eurh-hhhhh' – like the murmur Antony Worrall Thompson makes when he eats. I don't know why; you'd have to ask Antony.

Music! I need music. Throughout my life, it's been there for me. Divorced from Carol? Chicago all day long. Got me a pay rise? It's Haddaway for the drive home.[137] Kids' birthday party? Hands up who's heard of Dire Straits!

---

137 Full disclosure. In 2008 I spotted Haddaway in a hotel steam room. I strode over, introduced myself and said I wanted him to sing on a jingle I'd written. The sessions went badly, and it was only when I visited the same hotel and saw him dredging the pool that I realised he wasn't Haddaway, just a man who worked for Jurys Inn.

I'm down to the last 3 per cent of battery life, so I quickly look on my iPhone for the playlist I've called Alan's Belters. But Alan's Belter's isn't there. Nothing is. I curse myself for asking my assistant to update iTunes.[138] She's deleted everything so that there's only one track in the entire library, which – inexplicably – is a voice memo of her attempting to sing 'I Dreamed a Dream'.

After dreaming a dream in which I summarily dismiss her, I limp onwards. Fine, I think, I shall provide my own music, and I brainwave the idea of singing a song into my phone and playing it on a loop to stop me getting out of breath.

I begin: 'Rising up, back on the street. Did my time, took my chances. Went the distance, now I'm back on my feet. Just a man and his will to survive. It's the . . .'

'Dad?'

'Fernando?'

In my confusion – and by now I'm very, very confused – I've called my son instead of recording a voice memo.

'Jesus. It's half one. I've only just got the baby to sleep.'

'Ah. Little baby.' I often say this when someone mentions a baby and I can't think what to say. Then I add, 'Is he OK? I've love to meet him one day. And your lovely wife . . .'

'India.'

I exhale with sudden relief. I was *this* close to calling her Africa.

Fernando pauses. And I know that if he doesn't want me

---

138 Six months ago, she didn't even know what it was. I asked her if she'd heard of iTunes and she suggested 'Bright Eyes' and 'For Your Eyes Only'. Such a stupid woman.

to meet the baby, it's because Carol helps out with the infant and would have a few things to say. I spare his awkwardness by changing the subject.

'Fernando. If I died would you honour me by walking in my footsteps?'

'Would I what?'

Silence. The battery's gone. I look up and realise I've lost my bearings.

I turned landwards off the coastal road . . . but then what? All I know is that it's very dark and I'm in some kind of rural wilderness.

***

It's three hours later and I haven't dared to move. I feel woozy. I've walked a double marathon since I last sat down, and my foot is throbbing like a frog's neck. This is very much a survival situation[139] and I need to take some action. I lurch

---

139 This isn't the first time I've been in a survival situation. A few years ago I was hiking through some dense forest when my compass broke and I became lost. Without access to a satellite phone I was forced to launch an emergency flare, but when no one responded I was left with no choice but to search for civilisation on my own. I survived on foraged raspberries until, after what seemed like an eternity, I stumbled through the undergrowth into a clearing that contained a business park. Battered and thirsty, I entered the office of a recruitment agency and said, 'I'm Alan Partridge, I've been lost for four hours.' And they sat me down and called me a taxi. As I waited, I watched the news on TV and realised that during my ordeal there had been a minor cabinet reshuffle, and I'd had *absolutely no idea*. An intern gave me a machine coffee and I just burst into tears and held her hand.

around the wasteland like an absolute idiot. I hold out my arm to steady myself and find myself clinging to a piece of taut, metal bramble. I steady myself and – WAIT A MINUTE! Bramble isn't metal! It's almost always a twiggy substance, similar to wood. So what the hell am I holding on to?

I don't know what time it is, but the morning has just started to gloam, offering the smallest glimmer of half-light. I allow my eyes to squint, the bony caves of my eye sockets narrowing just enough for me to make out my fingers, gripping a fence-like structure (a fence). I'm at a fence. A sign says 'Nuclear Installations Act 1965, Licensed Site Boundary'.

I realise what this means just as my knees crumple like the Side Impact Protection System of a Volvo. I fall to the floor, holding onto the fence like a Great Escaper at the end of *The Great Escape*. I'm almost there! I've made it to the perimeter bramble of the power station. The wilderness I'd encountered was the Dungeness National Nature Reserve, which sits right next to the power station. I just need to climb over the fence and walk to the building itself . . . Suddenly, a noise.

I turn my head, at speed, eager to see who this way comes. Coming this way through the darkness is a hooded individual, moving at pace over the grass. Below the hem of the black cloak I can make out a pair of hiking boots. Suddenly, the becowled figure lifts the hood off and I see who it is.

'Julia?'

She turns and smiles. It's Julia Bradbury.

'Alan!' She approaches me and kisses me full on the

mouth. Steady on, Julia – you're married! You only gave birth to twin girls a year ago.[140] She disengages.

'What are you doing here?' I ask.

'It's a new series of walks I'm doing,' she says. '*Station to Station*. Started at the nuclear plant at Seascale in Cumbria and ended up here.'

'You've come all the way from Cumbria? You must be exhausted.'

'Not really,' she says. 'It's probably one of the easiest things I've ever done.'

'Same here,' says another voice. 'And I've rambled from Scotland.'

I look round and see two other hooded figures, heads bowed, like witches on a heath, or pensioners on a heath. The nearest figure lifts off her hood to reveal her face and the glossiest of glossy hair. It's Clare Balding.

'You've come from Scotland?' I say.

'Yep. Piece. Of. Piss.'

'And I'm Michael Portillo,' says the third hooded figure, removing the hood of his cloak.

I rub my eyes. 'Michael? Why are *you* dressed as a witch? You're not even a woman.'

'No, but I'd like to be,' he says, unbuttoning his shirt and pushing his flabby pecs together to make it look like a lady's cleavage. 'By the way, I walked from Vienna. I didn't even get the train. And I cannot believe how straightforward it was.'

---

140 I always like to Wikipedia my fantasy women. Just so that, however involved the thoughts become, there aren't any nasty surprises further down the line.

'You look like shit, Alan,' says Julia. 'Why are you here?'

'Oh, I'm walking in the footsteps of my father . . .'

'Quadriplegic, was he?' sniggers Portillo, nodding at my slumpage, and straight away I regret sending him a cake when he lost his seat in 1997.

'I'm just having a rest actually, Michael,' I say, trying to get up. But my legs are weak and I cannot, so I do not.

'See you later, then,' say the three celebrity travellers in unison, their voices harmonising like a barbershop quartet, if one of the barbers was off ill and two of them were female.

'What? Wait!' I say. But on they ramble. 'Please! I don't want to be left behind! I don't want to be left behind! Don't leave me behind!'

But they don't turn back and are soon disappearing into the murk, until even the shimmer of Balding's superb hair has gone from view. I roll onto my back and close my eyes in anguish, like a dying soldier in Vietnam or a tired soldier in Helmand Province. I lie there, eyes closed, listening to the sound of the sea – which I have to say is one of the most boring sounds there is – until I become aware that I am bathed in a warm light. I force my eyes open and there, standing over me, is a shepherd.

'You all right, mate?'

'Yes, thank you. I'm just tired.'

'Have some water,' he says as he helps me up. 'Got a full grail here.' I dust myself off as his sheep take turns to jump the fence in the middle of the field, and I am about to take a sip but it smells alcoholic, so I don't bother. I'm not going through that again. He'll probably twoc my shoes like his associate did all those days ago.

I try again to walk, wincing at the pain as I place my weight onto my fetid foot.

'Here, let me . . .' He reaches out to touch me but I shrink back. I once saw a *Crimewatch* where a guy got pally with a dog walker and then the dog walker put his hand down the man's trousers and told him not to tell anyone.

'It's OK,' the shepherd says. 'I heal the cripples. It's what I do.'

'Yeah, when you're not wrangling sheep on radioactive scrubland . . .'

'Why are you even doing this, Alan?'

I sigh and turn back. 'It's a long story, but I'm basically honouring the memory of my dead dad.'

'Try honouring yourself for once,' he says. 'Dad almighty, you deserve it!'

'How do you know?'

'I know loads,' he replies. 'Think about it, Alan. I am someone you're sure to have heard of.'

And with that, this kindly shepherd stands still and extends his arms out, making a capital 'T' shape. I smile. I *love* games like this. Hmmm . . . T.

'Teddy Thomas!' I proffer.

He smiles benignly, shaking his head.

'No, Tinie Tempah. Tommy Trinder! I know it's not Tanita Tik—'

He butts in. 'This isn't a 'T' shape. It's meant to be a crucifix.'

'Right. Why?'

'Because I am Jesus Christ, the Son of God.'

I am stunned. But only for a moment.

'Ah, now. Settle an argument,' I say. 'You're actually an Arab, aren't you?'

'Beg your pardon?'

'You're an Arab. Factually speaking.'

'No.'

'You are! You're an Arab!'

***

'You're an Arab! An Arab! An Arab!'

I'm slapped sharply to the face. I instinctively lash out, connecting with a forearm smash to the Son of God's nose. I regret that He'd put me in a position where a forearm smash was necessary, but even members of the Holy Trinity can overstep the mark.

Another slap. My eyes open. I realise now that I'm not in the Dungeness National Nature Reserve but on a hospital bed, and that I haven't assaulted Christ, but a nurse (a male one).

'You're an Arab . . .' I mumble to no one.

'Not me, friend,' said the wounded nurse (who was black, not that it matters). 'I'm from Bermuda.'

I have awoken in a bed at the William Harvey Hospital in Ashford. I'll cut to the chase because hospital stories are uniformly boring. ('Oh, please,' I always say in a voice dripping with sarcasm, 'tell me more about how long you had to wait in A&E, or about the time you were in a bed next to an old man who kept pulling his catheter out, or how your wife was in labour for fifty-six hours and there were complications so it was touch and go for a while and you genuinely thought you'd have to bring up baby on your own. Tell me more because it's sooooo interesting.')

So I shan't bore you with the humdrum, other than to say that my foot had become very badly infected and left me semi-conscious (at best). I was found babbling incoherently about struggling to find a terrestrial broadcaster, asking seemingly no one whether God thought I should take my walk directly to Netflix.

I'm placed on an antibiotic drip, given a tetanus shot and fluids, and told I should be fine. My next of kin (my assistant, through expediency rather than affection, I assure you) is in the car, on the way to collect me.

'The walk,' I say. 'The walk.'

'You're not walking anywhere, Alan. Look at your foot.'

I look down, cursing the NHS, when I realise they've cut my sock and training shoe off with shears because the foot was so badly swollen. They had to drain the foot, which isn't a phrase I've ever hankered to hear.

Some time later I ask if I can go and have a cigarette, please. Once outside, I limp past the actual smokers to the back of the building and, at the given time, my assistant pulls into the car park. Naturally, she screeches in in second and I wonder how long she's been in that gear.

It's 7 a.m. on Monday morning and I clamber into the passenger seat. The ruse has worked quite superbly. I don't even smoke!!

'Take me to North Norfolk Digital,' I tell her. 'And don't spare the horsepower.'

It's a pretty good line, but my assistant doesn't even titter. I smile to myself, in a funny kind of way reassured that, despite the hell I've been through, some things never change. She really is an appalling conversationalist.

My Journey

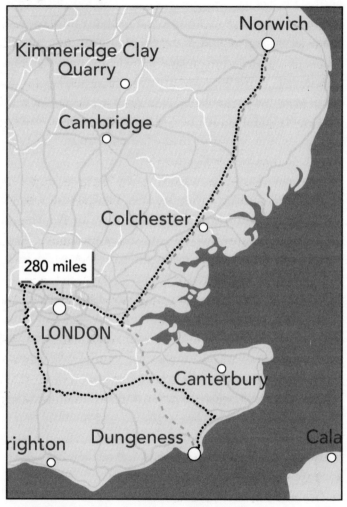

The 120-mile detour shown above was the result of an intended meeting with a well-connected agent, something my assistant now calls a 'wild goose chase'. Perhaps if she bothered to read up on wild geese, she'd know the down of these magnificent birds fetches up to $90 a pound, while the meat can feed a family of two for a whole weekend. Sounds like a pretty worthwhile pursuit to me, but there you go.

***

It's three hours later and I'm back on air, with my slacks changed, pits deodorised and hair combed. My assistant spent the journey breathing condensation onto the inner windscreen, but she looked after me, bless her, helping me to remove my healthy shoe and, since my hamstrings had tightened, washing my feet and legs before socking my feet back up.

The record I'm playing finishes.

'That was the Flying Pickets,' I say, 'dedicated to my assistant, [her name], a woman who, unlike pickets, is happy to work at the National Minimum Wage – a not unbusty sixty-nine-year-old spinster who's frumpy, dumpy and grumpy.'

'Sounds like three dwarves,' suggests Sidekick Simon.

'It does!' I agree. 'And from a distance she does look like three midgets huddled in her dead mum's coat.'

There's a blub, blub, blub, blub of bubbles in liquid, and I shoot a look to Sidekick Simon, who's been told time and again to go outside if he wants to drink from his water bottle. But his hands are empty and I remember I'm broadcasting while hooked up to a saline drip.

Simon starts to ask about my walk and tries to commiserate me on my agonising failure.

I tell him there was no failure.

He says that's not what he heard.

And I tell him, well, he heard wrong, then. I went right up to the fence. I touched it.

He sniggers again, and suggests that is like saying you

visited New York when you were turned away at the airport by US Customs.

That's a bit rich, I tell him, seeing as he's never been to America.

He says he is a bit rich, thanks, because he won £100 betting against me finishing it.

I tell him it's a good thing too because everyone knows he's the lowest-paid member of staff at the station by a distance, and he could probably use that money to pay for a haircut.

Zinger! I thwack my fingers together like a gangland black chap and spin round on my office chair, but I've forgotten I'm connected to the saline drip, and the tubing coils around my neck like a skinny, see-through python. Unable to breathe, I signal for Simon to continue, and he completes the link for me and then helps me destrangle myself.

I let his insubordination go, knowing full well I'll get him later in the men's by gently pushing him against a urinal while he pees. That is until I realise the drip qualifies me for access to the disabled toilets. I hole up there instead, just enjoying the space and letting my weary body slump against the leather back pad of the higher-than-usual toilet seat. I close my eyes and sleep, only emerging when a more visibly disabled visitor bangs on the door and asks if they can do toilet.

***

It's Friday and I no longer require the drip, so I leave it outside the front door of a residential home for the elderly with a note saying, 'From a kindly benefactor'.

Before what promises to be another good show – a really good one, fantastic actually – I've come to the swimming pool, not to get myself in QSPC this time but because I remember that a hydrotherapist I once interviewed (Annabel Swanswim) uses the pool on Fridays, and I'm hoping she can tell me more about using the warmth and weightlessness of the pool to aid my rehabilitation. My body is, in the wise words of Billy Ray Cyrus, 'achy, breaky'.

My foot is still very swollen and the wound hasn't fully closed up. I know this calls for a verruca sock but the foot is far too swollen to fit one, so I've opened out three hot water bottles using a pair of scissors and, with the help of gaffer tape, I've clad my foot in the bottles' rubber pelt to create a hardy, if quite heavy, verruca boot.

I lower myself into the water and slosh around for a while, letting the warm water lap at my back, flank and tits. And then I hear: 'Morning.'

My blood runs cold. I recognise that voice. It's my swimming nemesis, Dawn. I don't deign to reply. Indeed, I rarely deign much at all. Guess I'm not much of a deigner. Instead I seethe at her silently.

'You've got a welly on.'

For a terrible, terrible, *terrible* split second, I convince myself that a 'welly on' is pensioner slang for an erection. I surreptitiously paw at my Speedos to flatten the boner, but there is none, and then I realise she's referring to my improvised footwear.

'It's not a welly,' I mutter. 'It's a verruca boot.'

'Do you have verrucas?'

I'm not even answering that so, just as I did all those weeks ago, I allow myself to sink underneath the water, the most dramatic of exits, although my verruca boot's buoyancy means my left leg does stick out of the water.

But then, from within my watery lair, I hear a commotion. I resurface like a flesh-coloured Trident.

'Oh! Oh! Oh dear!' From the fuss she's making you'd think she was being dragged under by a Great White (shark, not man). She's not. Glancing at this silly woman, I realise that she's merely let go of her yellow nose clip. And – oh Jesus Christ, no – it's floating towards me.

I do my best to ignore it, but it's bee-lining right at me. Using my arms like a graveside soil-bulldozer, I try to create a tsunami that will surge the clip back towards her, but it merely bobs over the top of it and keeps coming for me.

In the end I have no choice. I gingerly reach for it and fish it out between my forefinger and thumb. Eurgh, this is, like, *so* gross.

I dangle it in Dawn's direction and she smiles at me and takes it, but rather than a clean pass, she clasps my whole hand, in a grandmotherly way. I meet her eye.

'Are you all right?' she asks.

Well, it all comes out. I tell her about my father, about the walk, about the hopes I had to monetise the journey through a TV and book deal, about Harvey 'Asshole' Kennedy, about my wound, the infection, and how, finally, I too failed, coming up metres short, just as my father had done.

When I finish speaking there's a silence, broken only by the sound of another boy doing a bomb. She smiles at me and I feel tears pricking in my eyes. I sink back into the water so that the tears can mingle with it and no one will be able to tell if I'm weeping or not.[141]

I then swim away, holding my breath until I reach the side, where I slink out of the pool and away.

I shower, dress and comb quickly and efficiently, and after rolling up my trunks into a towel like a Speedo sausage roll, I make for the exit.

But as I stride to the street, quite slowly as I've not been able to remove my verruca boot, I'm aware of someone watching me. Across the car park I see Dawn, this time in clothes. She holds up a hand by way of a wave, and I do the same, our hands motionless, fifty yards apart, like it's a prison visit and we're on either side of very, very thick glass.

She unlocks her car, opens the door and gestures towards it.

'WHAT?' I shout.

'Come on,' she says. 'I'll take you.'

***

Two and a half hours later (boy, does she drive faster than my assistant), I'm at the Dungeness Power Station Visitor Centre. I called in sick to North Norfolk Digital, knowing that Simon would get to take the reins. Once this would have made me convulse with physical sickness, but now I feel OK with it. He's a good man and deserves his chance (for a day).

Dawn and I spend a pleasant couple of hours learning all about this fascinating provider of electricity. Apparently,

---

141 A technique I pioneered some years ago called Shortburst Underwater Crying.

Dungeness was the first Advanced Gas-cooled Reactor to begin construction in the UK and supplied a total of 1050 MW to the national grid, and it isn't expected to be decommissioned until 2028.

'I'll be dead by then!' laughs Dawn, and I tell her that's nonsense, but it probably isn't. We stroll the site, enjoying a quite spellbinding day thanks to the use of interactive models, touch-screen computers and information panels that explain how electricity is generated in EDF Energy power stations, while also touching on safety on site, radiation and that old bugbear – nuclear waste!

The only downside is that the visitor centre is located within Dungeness 'B' power station, which wasn't open when my father secured an interview here. His job, had he got it, would have been at the now-closed Dungeness 'A', so I'm not really any closer to completing the journey.

However, after a few phone calls (in which I'm forced to throw my weight around a little), we're granted special access to the site so that I can walk up to the building and touch the front door. Dawn needs a little reassurance (a *lot* of reassurance) that she's not going to get radiation poisoning, but soon my kindly geriatric swim-buddy and I are on our way.

As we take the final few steps of my remarkable walked odyssey I feel the hand of history on my shoulder. For at this moment I am reaching out across time and space, back, back and back some more to the day in April 1965 on which my father mysteriously failed to reach this very place. You'd expect tears at this point, but it's when I begin to think about him – to *really* think about him – that something suddenly becomes clear. I feel an overwhelming urge to speak to Father directly.

Dawn is near so I lower my voice. I have grown genuinely fond of her and am touched by the way she's helped me, but at the end of the day she's a pensioner I met in a swimming pool, and I feel it's important not to lose sight of that. I rest my head against the power station. 'Father, it's me. It's Alan. May I please say something to you? I've always tried to give you the benefit of the doubt, to tell myself you were just misunderstood, but now I realise . . .'

Dawn pipes up to say that she's getting cold, having not brought a coat (a fairly basic error). I tell her to sit in the car, then, and turn back to my father/the wall.

'Now I realise you weren't misunderstood. You were just – on balance – not a nice man. Because I was a good little boy and you were really nasty to me. And I've never said this to anyone before, but . . .'

Dawn asks if I've got the car keys. It's quite an odd thing to say, I tell her, because it's her car. She apologises and shuffles off. I turn back to my father/the wall.

'I've never said this to anyone before: it was me who daubed the word "idiot" on your car that time. And it was also me who used to put the dead flies in your underpants drawer. I know you were probably only nasty to me because your dad was nasty to you.[142] And maybe I've even been nasty to my own kids from time to time, although they weren't entirely blameless (Fernando was a liar and Denise could be quite sneaky).

---

142 He worked at the docks. You get the picture.

'But you know something?' I smile, looking into his/the building's eyes. 'The generosity of a pensioner I met in a swimming pool, and to a lesser extent something Christ said to me, has made me decide to break that cycle. From now on I'm going to start being a little bit nicer to people. And maybe they'll be nicer to someone else. And that person will be nicer to someone else. And perhaps in some small way I can make things a little bit better for everyone.'

I pat the wall of the power station three times like it's my father's jowl and turn to walk away, but then, just like in the movies, I have a final thought and turn back. 'That said, although I initially started this walk to honour you, I've changed my mind now. You never managed to get all the way here but I have, and that means I'm better than you and, ultimately, the winner. Because you are nobody and I am Alan Partridge – Nomad.'

And with that, we get back into Dawn's 1.2-litre Volkswagen Polo and pull away into the dusk of this most nuclear of days. Goodbye.

31.

EPILOGUE

***

BUT QUESTIONS REMAINED. Why had my father failed to make it to his Dungeness interview? What had befallen him that day? These questions still hung in the air like the smell of sausage fat, long after the cooked breakfast has been eaten and the dishwasher stacked.

And so, using the money that I refused to pay to my branding consultant, I hired a team of investigators, diligent students from the University of East Anglia, who trawled visitor records and official correspondence from the power station.

They learnt that my father *had* actually made it to the interview but performed exceptionally badly and hadn't made it to the next round. It seems he fabricated the letter concerning his failure to attend because he didn't want his family and friends to realise how thick he was. And he took this dark secret to the grave with him (along with an envelope of his premium bonds – never known why).

And the blood on the receipt? Nothing more, it seems, than a very bad nose bleed.

As for Dawn, she's now on the payroll. I've made her my assistant's assistant, and although my assistant isn't that happy about it, it's a setup that I like. I call them the Golden Girls! Anyway, I think that's everything. All right, then. Thank you.

ALSO BY THIS AUTHOR

***

A Funny Thing Happened on the Way to the Stadium to Alan Partridge by Alan Partridge (1992)

Bouncing Back by Alan Partridge (2002)

Forward Solutions: An Imbecile's Guide by Alan Partridge (YTBP)[143]

I, Partridge: We Need to Talk About Alan by Alan Partridge (2011)

Planning Application for Single-storey Extension to Rear of Domestic Dwelling by Alan Partridge (2012)

I Wish to Make a Complaint: Collected Funny TripAdvisor Reviews by Alan Partridge (YTBP)

From the Quill of a Partridge . . . A Poetry Compendium by Alan Partridge (YTBPITUK)[144]

---

143 Yet to Be Published.
144 Yet to Be Published in the UK.

INDEX

***

---

145 There now follow five empty pages. Why? Well, it's all to do with *offset printing*. Offset print hardback books are made up of 'signatures', large folded sheets that form 8, 16, or 32 consecutive pages that are then mechanically folded and cut for binding. This is called an *even working*. Books printed in this manner will always have a number of pages that is a multiple of the number in such a signature; in this case sixteen. That's unavoidable.

I encroached ten pages into a fresh signature and that meant there were six fallow pages left over (sixteen minus ten being six). But what can I do? Cut ten pages worth of copy to avoid starting a signature? No chance. Not going to happen, mate. I've cut too much as it is. Bulk it up it with filler about walking, loft insulation or offset printing? Not my style. Say nothing and avoid drawing attention to it? No, I will do none of those things.

Instead, I give these pages over to you, the reader to record any ideas, feelings or fantasies that occur as you read. If this has become a GCSE set text, teachers may use the pages to map out lesson plans.

NOTES

NOTES

NOTES

NOTES

NOTES